WALKING ON THE
AMALFI COAST

About the Author

Gillian Price was born in England but moved to Australia when young. After taking a degree in anthropology and working in adult education, she set off to travel through Asia and trek the Himalayas. The culmination of her journey was Venice where, her enthusiasm fired for mountains, the next logical step was towards the Dolomites, only hours away. Starting there, Gillian is steadily exploring the mountain ranges and flatter bits of Italy and bringing them to life for visitors in a series of outstanding guides for Cicerone.

When not out walking and taking photos with Nicola, her Venetian cartographer husband, Gillian works as a translator and freelance travel writer (www.gillianprice.eu). An adamant promoter of the use of public transport to minimise impact in alpine areas, Gillian is an active member of CAI, the Italian Alpine Club, and the Outdoor Writers and Photographers Guild, the OWPG.

Other Cicerone guides by the author

Walking in the Dolomites
Walking in the Central Italian Alps
Walking in Tuscany
Walking in Sicily
Shorter Walks in the Dolomites
Treks in the Dolomites: Alta Via 1 and 2 (co-author)
Walking on Corsica
Trekking in the Apennines. Grande Escursione Appenninica, GEA
Through the Italian Alps. Grande Traversata delle Alpi, GTA
Across the Eastern Alps: E5
Gran Paradiso: Alta Via 2 Trek and Day Walks
Italy's Sibillini National Park
Walks and Treks in the Maritime

WALKING ON THE AMALFI COAST

by
Gillian Price

2 POLICE SQUARE, MILNTHORPE, CUMBRIA LA7 7PY
www.cicerone.co.uk

Text and photographs © Gillian Price 2010
Maps © Nicola Regine 2010

ISBN-13: 978 1 85284 591 9

Printed by KHL Printing, Singapore

A catalogue record for this book is available from the British Library.
All photographs are by the author unless otherwise stated.

Dedication

For sunny, sun-loving Pamela

Acknowledgements

Anna Z came adventuring again, facing up to wrong turns and knee-bashing
descents (and she still invites us to dinner). Local expert Giovanni Visetti deserves
recognition for his tireless efforts in encouraging walking in these superb areas.

Advice to Readers

Readers are advised that while every effort is made by our authors to ensure
the accuracy of guidebooks as they go to print, changes can occur during
the lifetime of an edition. Please check Updates on this book's page on
the Cicerone website (www.cicerone.co.uk) before planning your trip. It is
also advisable to check information such as transport, accommodation and
shops locally. Even rights of way can be altered over time. We are always
grateful for information about any discrepancies between a guidebook and
the facts on the ground, sent by email to info@cicerone.co.uk or by post to
Cicerone, 2 Police Square, Milnthorpe LA7 7PY, UK.

Front cover: Capri's magnificent Faraglioni

CONTENTS

Legend

═══════	sealed road	•	town, village
┅┅┅O┅┅┅	railway	🏰	tower, castle
──────────	walk route	†	church, chapel, shrine, cross
....	walk variant	🚠	cable-car
▲	crest, mountain peak	🚡	chair lift
︵	stream, river	Ⓢ Ⓕ	walk start/finish
•1380m j'n	spot height at junction	↘	walk direction

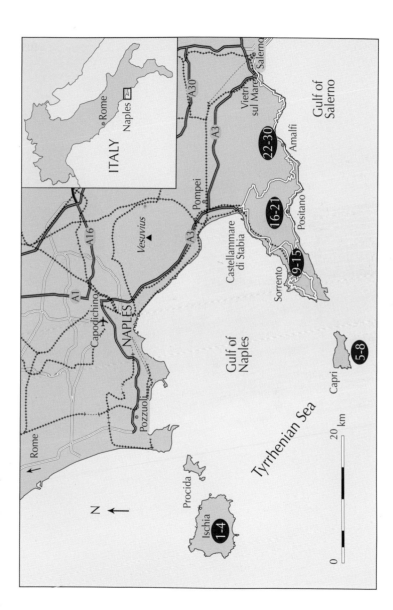

Lovely old houses are passed early on (Walk 4)

INTRODUCTION

Know'st thou the land where the lemon-trees bloom,
Where the gold orange glows in the deep thicket's gloom,
Where a wind ever soft from the blue heaven blows,
And the groves are of laurel and myrtle and rose?
   JW Goethe (1785)

Oh no, yet another 'unbeatable' walk. I'm running out of five-star adjectives.
   Fraught guidebook author after a walk on the Amalfi Coast (2009)

The Tyrrhenian Sea in southern Italy is an area of dramatic coastal scenery, none more so than in the Gulfs of Naples and Salerno where all the action in this book takes place. No number of dazzling glossy travel brochures or rave accounts from friends can prepare you for these sensational places and their natural beauty. There's the picture-perfect island of Capri, once the playground of pleasure-seeking Roman emperors, and contrasting Ischia, land of ancient volcanoes. Across the gulf the rugged Sorrento peninsula is lapped by sparkling turquoise water and criss-crossed by a great web of age-old mule tracks. Inland rises its mountainous backbone, the Monti Lattari, soaring to spectacular heights.

The steep southern edge goes by the name of the Amalfi Coast, incomparably beautiful and famous the world over. Settlements from the medieval era with outstanding architectural and artistic features perch on precipices high over the sea. Arable land being in short supply, over the centuries the ingenious inhabitants have painstakingly built up breathtaking sequences of stone retaining walls to support terraced vineyards and lemon orchards.

All this is great news for walkers, as the ancient network of routes leads across a range of stunning landscapes. A sense of wonder takes over each time you step out. The crowds and hustle of the coast are left quickly behind, and in their place are soothing green landscapes with masses of wild flowers and aromatic herbs, not to mention inspirational panoramas. This is a veritable paradise for walkers of all abilities and levels of experience.

The heritage of mule tracks linking the villages dotted over the mountainous peninsula and islands are an open invitation to visitors interested in exploring this beautiful region on foot. Routes in this guide follow country lanes as well as paved and

The beautiful setting of the
Sentiero degli Dei (Walk 18)

stepped knee-testing ways shared at times with herders, farmers and their mules loaded with firewood or freshly harvested lemons. On many occasions there are walkers-only paths across flowered hillsides thick with Mediterranean plants, exquisite wild orchids, lush green woods and jungle-like valleys. Pilgrims' routes lead to revered sanctuaries and goat tracks cross volcanic terrain.

FLOWERS AND PLANTS

Wherever you go in this magical part of the world you'll be walking through a garden of herbs and blooms. Easily recognisable are wild thyme, oregano and huge bushes of rosemary, used generously in the local kitchens. Commonly smelled long before it's seen is wild garlic, whose pretty milk-white flowers flourish in crannies on old masonry. The feathery lilac-tipped white blooms of the wandering caper vine sprout from stone walls and abandoned buildings. (The edible part is the bud itself, which can be salted or preserved in vinegar.)

Wild flower lovers visiting in spring and summer will have a field day. For starters the array of orchids is simply breathtaking: the early purple and insect orchids galore, the sombre burgundy serapias, and even the handsome *Orchis italica*, its pale pink blooms resembling little men (with no clothes on). Further bright splashes of rainbow colour in meadows and grassland are provided by carmine gladiolus, scarlet poppies and rich yellow broom.

Sun-baked hillsides are the perfect habitat for Mediterranean species such as rock roses (*Cistus*) whose delicate papery petals come in pastel pink and white. A common seaside delight with

Rock roses

Rock roses

Purple orchid

Serapias orchid

Orchis italica

Prickly pear flower

Curry plant

Anthyllis barba-jovis

unassuming woolly yellow flowers is called everlasting. A symbol of eternal love, its scientific name *Helichrysum* derives from the Greek for 'sun' and 'gold'. Its silvery elongated leaves conjure up oriental spices when rubbed, hence the nickname 'curry plant'. Renowned in antiquity for its medicinal properties, it was used for treating a wide range of ailments from coughs and migraines to asthma and rheumatism.

Tree spurge or *Euphorbia* rates a special mention. An attractive shrub that comes in a range of varieties, its fleshy green foliage assumes beautiful copper hues in late summer. However, be aware that it contains a toxic latex, an irritant to skin and eyes alike. Curiously it is an effective remover of warts and calluses and was once used for stunning fish before trapping them.

Not dissimilar in appearance, although much smaller and widely

11

Lemons flourish on the Amalfi Coast

used in cooking, is succulent rock samphire, called 'sea fennel' in Italian for its digestive properties. An attractive white convolvulus (*Convolvulus cneorum*) or silverbush is also common, although this name is also confusingly applied to the spectacular shiny-leaved seaside bush *Anthyllis barba-jovis*, the 'beard of Jupiter'.

The rare giant chain fern *Woodwardia radicans*, whose fronds grow up three metres long, survives in shady wooded reserves on the Amalfi Coast. The agave is another large plant – a monstrous cactus-like plant with ferocious spiked fleshy 'leaves' around the base of an extremely over-sized asparagus stem that sprouts gigantic blooms.

One unmistakable landmark plant found in abandoned fields is the prickly pear, a type of cactus also known by the colourful if misleading name of Barbary fig. It was allegedly introduced to Europe from South America by Christopher Columbus. It sports bright yellow or red paperish flowers protected by spines, as well as reddish-purple egg-shaped fruit, edible if not particularly tasty once all the insidious prickles have been carefully extracted.

Trees include the Mediterranean mainstay, the graceful olive, introduced to Italy by the ancient Greeks who developed it through grafting. In spring tiny creamy blooms appear. In late autumn the trees are hung with nets in readiness for the November harvest when the oil-rich fruit is shaken off.

Another typical tree is the carob, long appreciated for its nutritious fruits. Its leaves are shiny green and it bears ungainly lime green pods which darken to a chocolate colour late summer.

Last but definitely not least are the lemon trees, synonymous with the Sorrento peninsula and the Amalfi Coast. Painstakingly trained across wood frames and pergolas, they could almost be mistaken for vines, their big juicy fruit lobes hanging like grapes. They too are carefully covered with netting, but as protection against damage by hail and birds in the lead up to harvest.

WILDLIFE

Fossil remains of mammoth, prehistoric cave bears and even rhinoceros were unearthed on Capri in the early 1900s, and the rare protected

Mediterranean monk seal once swam off its coast. These days the fauna is mostly limited to birds and reptiles. Healthy colonies of seagulls gather on dizzy cliff tops, while the occasional bird of prey can be spotted hovering over open upland.

The creatures most commonly encountered on walks are lizards. Both iridescent green and lighter, tan brown, they laze on stone walls sunning themselves. A rustle of dry leaves and a dash to a tree is their typical reaction to the approach of outsiders. The clever gecko on the other hand is easier to see in the evening, crawling across walls close to bright lights, which attract insects it can prey on.

On Capri one of the Faraglione rock pinnacles boasts a rare blue lizard *Lacerta viridens faraglionensis*. According to local lore the creature

Green lizard

has assumed the colouring of the bright blue sea and sky around it!

Next comes the dung beetle. Industrious and ingenious, they free the fields and paths of droppings left by livestock by shaping the dung into huge balls which they then roll away in a comical sequence of moves, like a circus act. The beetles lay their eggs in this warm, nutritious compost.

Pretty butterflies enjoy the wealth of flowers by day, while on balmy summers evenings the flickering points of fireflies light up the bushes.

Snakes are not unusual, but none are poisonous. Cold-blooded creatures, they have a habit of sunning themselves on paths. If surprised – and just as frightened as you – they may lash out and bite, so give them time to escape. The attractive western whip snake comes in black-grey or yellow-green and can grow up to two metres in length.

On the list of potential 'nasties' are jellyfish, which come in pretty pink and purple hues in these waters. While not deadly they can inflict a very itchy sting and are best avoided! If stung, ask at a pharmacy (*farmacia*) for a suitable cream. Jellyfish are known as *medusa* in Italian.

EXPLORING AND BASES

Naples, or Napoli, is the capital of the Campania region and transport hub for all visitors thanks to its busy port, airport, rail and bus terminals. Should you need to stay there, you can't go wrong with B&B Bellini ☎ 081 0607338 www.bellininaples.com. Urban bedlam notwithstanding, this is a fascinating monumental city crammed with art, architecture and a history stretching back to the ancient Greeks. It enjoyed an extended period of glory as the headquarters of the Kingdom of Naples, then of the Kingdom of the Two Sicilies until Italian Unification in 1861. The metropolis is overlooked by brooding Vesuvius, the 1281m volcano responsible for burying Pompei and Herculanum with lava and ash in AD79.

To the west lie the Campi Flegrei (Phlegraean Fields, from the Greek 'burn'), where fuming sulphur emissions and seismic rumblings are ongoing, albeit minor. A short boat trip across the sea from the rocky headland 33km southwest of Naples is **Ischia**, a beautifully attractive mountainous island cloaked in green woodland and boasting an active volcanic past. The combination of long sandy beaches, thermal spas, affordable accommodation – and rewarding walking – make it a great holiday destination. The island's panoramic peak, Monte Epomeo, stars in Walk 1, while Walks 2 and 3 visit old craters and *fumarole* steam vents, and Walk 4 wanders through agricultural landscapes. The introduction to the Ischia section provides further information including suggestions for where to stay.

Shaped like a whale swimming west across the Gulf of Naples is incomparably divine **Capri**. A different

Ischia Porto

kettle of fish to laid-back Ischia, it has boasted sophistication and fashion since Roman times – not to mention outrageously high prices – and spectacular natural beauty accessible by way of a wonderful series of paths. The island is surprisingly mountainous, its limestone composition linking it with the Monti Lattari on the Sorrento peninsula to which it was attached in ancient times; nowadays it is 5.5km offshore. So beautiful is Capri that any walk is guaranteed to be rewarding and memorable.

Understandably the island receives colossal numbers of day visitors and tour groups who arrive by the boatload to admire the sights. A boat tour of the spectacular cliff perimeter is popular, via the Faraglioni stacks and the shimmering Grotta Azzurra – both of which can be admired on walks described here. Another popular pastime is to take the chair lift up the highest peak Monte Solaro, visited on foot in this guidebook. Walks 6, 7 and 8 begin at the town itself, while Walk 5 starts out at the landmark lighthouse on the northwestern headland. See the introduction to the Capri section for more information.

A seagull's glide from Capri, on the mainland, the Sorrento peninsula dips its big toe into the Tyrrhenian. That tip, the majestic Punta Campanella (visited on Walks 11–13), is the westernmost extremity of a rugged limestone range. The Monti Lattari rise above heavily wooded slopes to dramatic heights, peaking at 1444m with scenic Monte

15

Cruise liners moor off Sorrento

Sant'Angelo (Walk 9). On the northern coast, facing onto the Gulf of Naples, stands **Sorrento** itself, a very attractive town set atop dizzy cliffs over a bay where cruise liners jostle for moorings. Walk 10 is nearby. Geared to the needs of tourists it offers plenty of accommodation and facilities, and is a well-served transport hub for trains and ferries connecting with Naples, the islands of Ischia and Capri and the Amalfi Coast. An excellent network of buses fans out across the mountains to serve far-flung villages (see the Sorrento introduction for details).

The main road SS145 travels south through farmland green with crops and vines, in sight of the Gulf of Salerno via Sant'Agata sui Due Golfi then Colle San Pietro – Walks 14 and 15 are in the vicinity.

Offshore three legendary rock pinnacle islands stand out. Known as Li Galli, they were described by Homer as the place where Ulysses was tempted by the Sirens; nowadays they are surrounded by shipwrecks. In the days of the Republic of Amalfi, despotic doges would be exiled to their desolate shores. Later on, in the 1900s, Rudolf Nureyev made a home there.

From here on, things become seriously dramatic and spectacular. The road, now the SS163, a late 19th-century feat of engineering, cuts around awesome cliffs, announcing the start of the impossibly steep, world famous Costiera Amalfitana, Amalfi Coast. These southern reaches of the Monti Lattari range have been recognised by UNESCO as World Heritage since 1997, and rightly so.

Car drivers need to be prepared for countless narrow bends, limited visibility, cumbersome coaches, and lack of parking in the villages en route. Bottom line: take the bus!

The first settlement to be encountered is gorgeous, chic **Positano** clustered in a sheltered valley. A mosaic of colourful houses tumbles down steep mountainsides linked by a network of stepped lanes. With a good choice of accommodation and services, it is well connected by year-round bus and boat in summer. From Positano Walks 16 and 17 venture up through scenic villages clinging to mountainsides overhead.

On the main road 8km east is **Praiano**, much quieter and so a good alternative place to stay, and handy for Walks 19 and 20. Way above are Bomerano and Agerola, on the dizzy SS366 link road with the Gulf of Naples. This is the official start of the famous Sentiero degli Dei (Walk 18).

Back down on the Gulf of Salerno coast is a string of magical coves and inlets, many overlooked by picturesque Saracen watchtowers, erected in medieval days when pirate attacks were the flavour of the day. Walk 21 explores the area. See the Positano section introduction for more.

Amalfi is the next noteworthy port of call, a former maritime republic that rivalled even the mighty Venice in days long gone by. Fascinating cramped medieval quarters are squeezed into a valley mouth, cathedral and all! It makes an excellent base for Walks 22 and 23, and acts as a hub for useful bus routes, both local and long-distance.

Just around the corner is Atrani, squashed into a tiny corner over a bay (in a space so tiny that the road has to make use of a flyover!).

Almost overhead and reached by a near-vertical road is sophisticated **Ravello**, a rather different cup of tea. Easily reached by bus from Amalfi, it is the base for Walks 25 and 26. On an attractive peaceful promontory close by is Pontone, an old market village and the start of Walk 24.

A couple of kilometres on is the laid-back seaside resort of Minori and access to Walks 27 and 28, then neighbouring Maiori for Walk 30. Backing the narrowing coastal strip the terrain here becomes wilder, and

Basilica Santa Trofimena at Minori

17

Walk 29 visits an elevated mountain-top sanctuary.

During the final 20km, only a handful of settlements – namely Cetara and Vietri sul Mare – dot the steep coast before the SS163 concludes its arduous course at the bustling port city of Salerno, on the main railway line.

INFORMATION

Tons of information on where to stay, what to see and how to do it can be gleaned from the following Tourist Authorities:

Amalfi ☎ 089 871107
www.amalfitouristoffice.it
Capri ☎ 081 8370686
www.capritourism.com
Ischia ☎ 081 5074211/31
www.infoischiaprocida.it
Maiori ☎ 089 877452
www.aziendaturismo-maiori.it
Massa Lubrense ☎ 081 5339021
www.massalubrense.it
Naples ☎ 081 24577475
www.inaples.it
Positano ☎ 089 875067
www.aziendaturismopositano.it
Praiano ☎ 089 874557
www.praiano.org
Ravello ☎ 089 857096
www.ravellotime.it
Salerno ☎ 089 2592555
www.salernoturismo.it
Sant'Agata sui Due Golfi ☎ 081 5330135 www.santagatasuiduegolfi.it
Sorrento ☎ 081 8074033
www.sorrentotourism.com

GETTING THERE

Naples' airport is Capodichino, www.gesac.it. Situated 7km NE of the city, it has frequent bus links to the centre as well as handy direct shuttles to Sorrento by Curreri Viaggi ☎ 081 8015420 www.curreriviaggi.it.

Main line trains south of Rome stop at Napoli Centrale – timetables and online tickets at www.trenitalia.it. Next door is the Napoli Garibaldi station for the Circumvesuviana railway (www.vesuviana.it/web) that takes 1hr to travel around the gulf to Sorrento.

The majority of the ferries sailing to Sorrento, Ischia and Capri leave from Molo Beverello, a 15min city bus trip from the central station. An alternate embarkation point is Molo Mergellina, close to the railway station of the same name; there's also Pozzuoli mostly for vehicle transport. Salerno at the eastern extremity of the Amalfi Coast is another good embarkation point for routes along the entire peninsula. Travel is by fast passenger ferry (*aliscafo*) and leisurely ship (*traghetto*, which also transport cars). See Ferries below for more.

GETTING AROUND

Every single walk in this guide can be accessed by public transport, as indeed all the research was done. Services are reliable, punctual and very reasonably priced. Train, bus, ferry and even a chair lift and cable-car are used. Practical details are given at the beginnings of individual sections.

Car

A rental car is a mixed blessing. While on the positive side a car means you can nip over to your rented villa or out-of-the-way hotel at will, it's a bit of a nightmare when you need to park in a village or at a walk start. On the Amalfi Coast space is a premium and most roads are unbelievably narrow – you'll need nerves of steel when faced with a cumbersome tourist coach obliging you to reverse or hang a wheel over the edge while he squeezes past. Moreover it means an extra polluting vehicle in this divine region. It's preferable to entrust yourself to the local bus or taxi drivers who know every twist and turn of the road better than the backs of their hands. They are also surprisingly patient with visiting drivers who get themselves into sticky situations!

On the Amalfi Coast and Sorrento there is a charge for parking, so you'll need to buy a 'Park Card' from a tobacconist (*tabaccaio*) or newsagents (*giornalaio*), and display it on your windscreen.

Be warned that private vehicles cannot be taken onto the island of Capri at all. The neighbouring island of Ischia accepts them, however it is unnecessary in view of the excellent local transport.

Buses and Lifts

In general bus tickets must be purchased beforehand. They are usually available at tobacconists (recognisable by their black and white 'T' sign), cafés or newsagents displaying a 'biglietto' sign. Fares depend on the distance travelled. It's a good idea to buy tickets in advance for your return

Ticket booths at Positano ferry wharf

USEFUL EXPRESSIONS

Un biglietto/due biglietti per Amalfi per favore	One ticket/two tickets to Amalfi please
Andata	single
Andata ritorno	return
Quanto costa?	How much is that?
Grazie	Thank you
Prego	You're welcome

The following terminology may come in helpful in understanding timetables.

Cambio a ... /coincidenza	change at ... /connection
Estivo/invernale	summer/winter
Feriale	working days (Monday to Saturday)
Festivo	holidays (Sundays and public holidays)
Giornaliero	daily
Lunedì a venerdì/sabato	Monday to Friday/Saturday
Sciopero	strike
Scolastico	during school term

journey if you'll be boarding the bus in an outlying place. Multi-day tickets are always worth it. An example is the Unico Costiera pass sold for the Sorrento peninsula and Amalfi Coast: a single ticket costs €2 whereas a three-dayer is only €6.

Timetables are posted at most bus stops but it's advisable to get a copy from the tourist office or relevant website before setting out. See the individual section introductions for local details.

Ferries

A host of ferries fast and slow plies the islands and mainland, a delightful way to travel from one area to another. This is especially true for the Sorrento and Amalfi districts, where

coast-hugging shuttle ferries operate intensively from spring to autumn, though less frequently over the winter months. For routes and timetables see Medmar www.medmargroup.it, Caremar www.caremar.it, Alilauro www.alilauro.it, Volaviamare www.volaviamare.it, SNAV www.snav.it Alicost www.lauroweb.com/alicost.htm, Metro del Mare www.metrodelmare.com, Travelmar ☎ 089 872950 and Linee Marittime Partenopee ☎ 081 7041911.

Note that ferry schedules are occasionally disrupted and services cancelled by high seas though bad weather rarely lasts more than a day or two. Ferries from the mainland to the Ischia and Capri take between 20min and 90min depending on the ports you use and whether you go for a fast or slow service.

Organised Walking
Walking tours to the Amalfi Coast are organised by agencies many and varied from all over the world, several offering a self-guided option with ongoing luggage transport (www. piccolotours.com). As guides go, you'd be hard to better Giovanni Visetti, the leading local authority on the walking possibilities; he speaks excellent English (www.giovis.com).

WHEN TO GO

What a dilemma! The Amalfi Coast, Sorrento peninsula and the islands of Capri and Ischia are beautiful destinations at any time of year. Spring is warmly recommended for lovers of wild flowers and mild air temperatures. Midsummer (July–August) can be pretty hot, though sea breezes can usually be counted on along the coasts   Capri for one boasts a modest average of 23°C in the summer months. But be warned that this is high season when tour coaches clog the roads, and accommodation best booked in advance. Autumn brings crystal clear skies, russet colours in the woods and quieter paths. Winter can be superb with few other visitors and low season prices (and some hotel closures); however, strong winds and stormy conditions can lower temperatures dramatically so wrap up well. Notwithstanding this is the southern Mediterranean and freezing conditions are atypical.

Be aware (beware!) of the Italian public holidays when everywhere get especially crowded, traffic piles up and hotel prices soar. In addition to the Christmas, New Year and Easter periods, you may prefer to steer clear of 6 January, 25 April, 1 May, 2 June, 15 August, 1 November and 8 December.

For the region overall, temperatures average out as: 9°C Dec–Feb, 14°C March–May, 23°C June–Aug, 17.5°C Sept–Nov.

ACCOMMODATION

The choice of where to stay in this part of the world is immense. The range goes from multi-starred hotels all the way through to the odd hostel. Suggestions for the low to medium price ranges are given in the separate area sections, otherwise fuller listings can be consulted on tourist office websites (see Information above). Advance booking at hot spots such as Capri, Positano and Amalfi is warmly recommended in high season; a deposit is generally requested. On the other hand, out of season – such as the winter months – it's not unusual to be able to negotiate lower rates, though be aware that many places close up for prolonged periods.

Payment is accepted by credit card at big establishments, though family-run affairs prefer euros cash. While it's always inadvisable to carry

The cascade of houses at Positano and the amazing coast road

a large amount of cash on your person, don't rely on anywhere but the key towns to have an ATM.

English is widely spoken at the main tourist spots, though never assume this and always check with *Parla inglese?* (Do you speak English?). A sprinkling of Italian is highly desirable and all attempts will endear you to the locals. Say *'Pronto'* to start a phone call, then try with these when booking a room:

- *Buon giorno (Buona sera).*
  Cerco una camera matrimoniale (singola) con (senza) bagno per una notte (due notti) da oggi (domani).
  Good morning (evening). I'm looking for a double (single) room with (without) bathroom for one night (two nights) as from today (tomorrow).
- *Avete un lettino per un bambino?* Do you have a small bed for a child?
- *Avete qualcosa di più grande (economico)?* Do you have anything larger (cheaper)?
- *Arrivo stasera (domani).* I arrive this evening (tomorrow).

CULINARY DELIGHTS

This southern Italian region of Campania has superb food based on seasonally fresh local ingredients. A mouth-watering survey of dishes to look out for is given here. Walkers deserve a good feed after a day out in the open air!

Pomodoro (tomato) and luscious creamy mozzarella cheese, preferably made with *latte di bufala* (buffalo milk), easily top the produce list. They make a joint appearance with the help of aromatic basil on traditional Neapolitan pizza baked in wood-fired ovens.

Gnocchi alla sorrentina is a tasty filling opening course to a meal – a tomato and white cheese sauce melted over tiny delicate potato dumplings. *Scialatielli* means homemade pasta that comes in short cut segments – perfect with a spicy sauce of stewed aubergine (*melanzane*). *Maccheroni* on the other hand bear no resemblance to the stodgy excuse served as macaroni overseas. Often hand-made and slightly undercooked, *al dente*, varieties of *rigatoni* tubes or twisted *fusilli* retain their shape perfectly when accompanying all matter of fish and meat sauces.

On the fish front, restaurants will often serve the day's catch so ask what's on or check the blackboard menu. *Totani* are a type of calamari, stewed or tossed lightly with prawns and rocket. A traditional method is *Totani alla Praianese*, freshly fished and sautéed with potatoes. Any variety of pasta *alla pescatore* means with seafood.

On Ischia you'll be able to enjoy *Pasta con fagioli, cozze e provolone*, a winning combination of pasta with beans, mussels and melted provolone cheese. *Coniglio all'Ischitana* means rabbit stewed with garlic, tomato, white wine, chilli and herbs.

Capri has its famous *Insalata caprese*, namely mozzarella served with slices of fresh tomato and basil. Then there are fragrant *Ravioli alla caprese*, homemade pasta pockets filled with egg, parmesan, marjoram and caciotta cheese.

Non mangio né carne né pesce is Italian for 'I don't eat meat or fish', which is more helpful than telling people you're a vegetarian.

As far as drinks go, connoisseurs will enjoy delicious spring water flowing from village fountains during walks unless labelled *'non potabile'* (tap water is always safe to drink). Fresh orange juice from locally grown fruit and squeezed on the spot is simply delicious and widely on offer.

A number of wines, white in particular, hail from these fertile regions. From the outskirts of Naples come *Campi Flegrei* and *Greco di Tufo* and Ischia has a recommendable *Biancolella* with just a light hint of fizz. However production struggles to keep up with demand from visitors so you will often be drinking wines from other areas such as Puglia, which produces memorable *Falanghina*.

Stronger stuff comes as *nocino*, made from the famed Sorrento *noci* or walnuts. The fame of the delicate Limoncello liquor – served in thimble-size ice-frosty glasses – has already spread well from its home base on the Amalfi Coast. More delights come with citrus: desserts the ilk of *delizia al limone*, a soft dome of feather-light sponge with lemon cream. Watch out for *Babà al rhum,* syrupy sponge cones often served with cream. A time-honoured tart from Naples, baked to celebrate Easter but produced by all reputable *pasticcerie* year-round, is the *pastiera napoletana*, a sweet pie filled with a luscious mix of ricotta, chunks of

Limoncello and lemon soap on sale

candied orange and cooked wheat. *Biscotti all'amarena* are another treat, a glacéed pastry sandwich around an *amarena* cherry filling. Then there are shell-shaped, multi-layered *sfogliatelle* consumed oven-warm when the pastry is still chewy and the sweet cheese-fruit mixture fragrant.

As concerns picnic lunches, most neighbourhood grocery shops are usually happy to make up bread rolls (*panini*) filled with your choice of cheese (*formaggio*) or cold meat such as salami or ham (*prosciutto*), easy to order from unfailingly attractive counter displays.

Breakfast is a simple affair – most Italians take a coffee as *cappuccino* (with frothy milk) or *espresso* (black concentrated strong shot) standing up at the local café; usually accompanied by a *cornetto*, as the croissant is known in the Naples region. Hotels and B&Bs will offer the choice of tea as well, and provide bread, butter and jam, fruit juice and occasionally cereals if you're lucky.

WHAT TO TAKE

First and foremost don't forget sun protection in the shape of a hat, high factor cream and sunglasses which should be taken on every single walk in this guide. A bottle of drinking water is another essential; plastic mineral water bottles are perfect as they can be refilled.

Day gear can be carried in a small-sized pack. Shoulder and hand-held bags are not a good idea as it's safer to have hands and arms free while walking.

Footwear: if you prefer ankle support, then take lightweight trekking boots. Otherwise a decent pair of trainers or sports shoes will do fine as long as they have good grip and thickish soles to protect your feet from loose stones. Tempting though sandals may be, they're quite inadvisable for walking the paths described in this guide. However, having said that, be aware that most of the beaches consist of crippling black pebbles so do take a pair along if you intend to spend time basking in the sun and taking a dip. It goes without saying that swimming costumes are essential unless you plan a visit in midwinter.

Weatherproof gear including a lightweight jacket and rucksack cover is indispensable. Strong winds and rain are not uncommon. T-shirts are suitable during spring/summer, layered with a light sweater or shirt for cooler conditions. Shorts are fine for both sexes, though exercise discretion when visiting inland villages and towns.

Autumn/winter visitors should pack warm clothes – long trousers, fleece or pullover, hat and gloves.

A simple first aid kit is always a good idea, and should include a disinfectant for scratches and minor cuts as well as band aids and insect repellent. A whistle and headlamp or torch are important if calling for help in an emergency. A mobile phone can be useful for organisational purposes such as calling hotels, but don't rely on it in an emergency as the mountainous regions and sheltered coast do not have full signal coverage. Don't forget an adapter and recharger.

A camera and spare batteries are a must to capture all those wonderful landscapes.

MAPS

Sketch maps are provided alongside the walk descriptions in this guidebook. The idea is to provide as much useful detail and as many key landmarks as possible, space permitting. Acquiring a larger commercial map is also warmly recommended for identifying distant points of interest and for plotting your own routes.

One map that covers nearly all the walks in this guide is 'Monti Lattari, Penisola Sorrentina Costeria Amalfitana' 1:30,000 published by SELCA (www.selca-cartografie.it) and on sale locally. Its only drawbacks are the indistinct contour lines and the lack of detail in villages with their maze of alleys.

Several 1:10,000 *carta dei sentieri* walking maps (www.carteguide.com) are available locally. They show paths in greater detail, though the coverage means multiple maps are needed. Their downside is the incomprehensible dearth of landmarks and names. There are currently three useful

maps: 1 does Vietri sul Mare (close to Salerno) as far as Minori, 2 Maiori to Furore, and 3 covers Conca dei Marini to Positano.

Both the Ravello and Amalfi Tourist Offices have free maps showing walking routes in their districts.

The promontory centring on Massa Lubrense is covered by an excellent 1:18,000 map, available free of charge at the Tourist Office. Another clear one is the new 1:12,500 'Monte Faito & S. Angelo a Tre Pizzi'.

For Capri a decent if small map can be downloaded from the Capri Tourism website, www.capri tourism.com; it shows the paths used in Walks 5, 7 and 8, though not Walk 6. They've also put out a 1:10,000 map – available at €1. At the time of writing it needed updating as many key paths were missing. Otherwise Kompass do a good 1:7500 map 'Isola di Capri'.

Ischia is a bit of a no-man's land. Kompass has done 1:15,000 map n.680, easily the clearest on the market, however it too contains a number of unfortunate inaccuracies.

Walking maps are available from leading map suppliers in the UK such as Stanfords www.stanfords.co.uk or The Map Shop www.themapshop.co.uk and through Libreria Stella Alpina in Florence www.stella-alpina.com.

Italian terminology commonly found on maps can be found in English translation in Appendix A.

EMERGENCIES

For medical matters, EU residents need a European Health Insurance Card (EHIC), which has replaced the old E111. Holders are entitled to free or subsidised emergency treatment in Italy, which has an excellent national health service. UK residents can apply online at www.dh.gov.uk. Australia similarly has a reciprocal agreement – see www.medicareaustralia.gov.au.

Travel insurance to cover a walking holiday is also strongly recommended as costs in the case of rescue and repatriation can be hefty.

The following services may be of help should problems arise. Remember that calls made from a public phone require a coin or pre-paid card to be inserted, though no charge is made for short emergency numbers or those starting 800 which are toll-free.

- Polizia (police) ☎ 113
- Health-related emergencies including ambulance (*ambulanza*) and mountain rescue ☎ 118

'Help!' in Italian is *Aiuto!*, pronounced 'eye-you-tow'. *Pericolo* is 'danger'.

USING THIS GUIDE

The walks described in this guide have been selected for their suitability for a wide range of holidaymakers. There is something for everyone, from leisurely family strolls to strenuous climbs for experienced walkers who

A selection of typical path signs and map boards to keep an eye out for

want to scale the heights of panoramic peaks. Each walk has been designed to fit into a single day. This means carrying only a small day pack and being able to return to comfortable lodgings afterwards. Panoramic picnics are the norm, though many routes touch on cafés and restaurants where 'civilised' refreshment breaks can be enjoyed.

The excellent network of low-cost public transport on both land and sea in this region makes this possible, namely trains, buses, ferries and cable-car!

As a bonus, a delightful day out on the pathways can be followed up with a cooling swim in that sparkling sea that's been beckoning all day!

The walks are listed under five sections corresponding to geographical areas, namely Ischia, Capri, Sorrento, Positano and Amalfi. They include introductory sections where more local flavour and information of a practical nature is provided as well as accommodation information.

Each walk description is preceded by a heading containing the following essential data:

- **Walking time** – this does not include pauses for picnics, admiring views, photos and nature stops, so always add on a good couple of hours when planning your day. Times given during the description are partial (as opposed to cumulative).
- **Difficulty** – rated on a scale of 1–3. Grade 1 is an easy stroll on mostly flat ground, suitable for all. Grade 2 is a little strenuous, with reasonable distances and climbs/drops included. A basic level of fitness is required. Grade 3 means orientation issues may be involved,

The path through citrus orchards below Monte dell'Avvocata (Walk 29)

Gorgeous view across to the Monti Lattari from Capri

as well as exposure or arduous stretches. Experience and extra care are recommended.

- **Ascent/Descent** – the overall uphill/downhill covered on this itinerary.
- **Distance** – given in both kilometres and miles.

During the walk descriptions 'path' is used to mean a narrow pedestrian-only way, 'track' and 'lane' are unsurfaced but vehicle-width, and 'road' is sealed and open to traffic unless specified otherwise. Compass bearings are in abbreviated form (N, S, NNW and so on) as are right (R) and left (L). Reference landmarks encountered en route are in **bold** type, with their altitude in metres given as 'm', (100m=328ft).

As research proceeded with this guidebook some path signs were being installed along the Amalfi Coast,

so there may be the odd discrepancy. However in general there's very little waymarking so directions need to be followed carefully. Moreover things do change in rural Italy, landslips mean paths are re-routed and vegetation can smother little-used ways. Details that come to light following the publication of this guide will be posted under 'Updates' on this book's page on the Cicerone website (www. cicerone.co.uk).

DOS AND DON'TS

- Don't set out late on walks even if they're short. Always have extra time up your sleeve to allow for detours and wrong turns.
- Find time to get in decent shape before setting out on your holiday, as it will maximise enjoyment. The

29

wonderful scenery will be better appreciated in the absence of exhaustion, and healthy walkers will react better in an emergency.

- Don't be overly ambitious, choose itineraries suited to your capacity. Read the walk description before setting out.
- Stick with your companions and don't lose sight of them. Remember that the progress of groups matches that of the slowest member.
- Avoid walking in brand new footwear as they may cause blisters; on the contrary, leave those old worn out shoes in the shed as they may be unsafe on slippery terrain. Choose your footwear carefully. Comfort is essential.
- Check the weather forecast locally if possible and don't start out even on a short route if storms are forecast as paths can get slippery and mountainsides are prone to rockfalls in storms.

- Carry weatherproof gear at all times, along with food and plenty of drinking water.
- In electrical storms, don't shelter under trees or rock overhangs and keep away from metallic fixtures.
- **Do not** rely on your mobile phone as there may not be any signal.
- Carry any rubbish back to the village where it can be disposed of correctly. Even organic waste such as apple cores and orange peel is best not left lying around as it can upset the diet of animals and birds and spoil things for other visitors.
- Be considerate when making a toilet stop. Keep away from watercourses, don't leave unsightly paper lying around and remember that abandoned huts and rock overhangs could serve as life-saving shelter for someone else!
- Lastly, don't leave your common sense at home.

Looking across to Vesuvius from Sorrento

ISCHIA

Curious split boulder at Pellacchio (Walk 1).

INTRODUCTION

Laid-back, green and populous, Ischia is by far the largest island in the Gulf of Naples. Covering 47km² with a circumference of 39km, it has a resident population of 55,000. While proudly *ischitano*, it is also very Neapolitan in flavour – which translates into outgoing people, great wood-oven pizzas, and even the occasional rip-off.

The name Iscla, from the Latin for 'island', was reportedly first used in 813. However a much earlier appellation was Pithecussae, which means 'island of the monkeys'. The fact is that the inhabitants had abandoned their god-fearing ways and resorted to brigandry. So irritated was he by their misbehaviour that Zeus, king of the Gods, turned them into apes! Another version links the name to 'makers of Greek vases'.

Geologically speaking the island is of igneous origin, a natural ancient progression of the mainland, formed 150,000 years ago as the result of seismic activity. Its 40 or so volcanoes produced lava flows and accompanying earthquakes which continued to devastate its settlements and shape its varied history up until the 1800s. Place names on the island reflect the geological

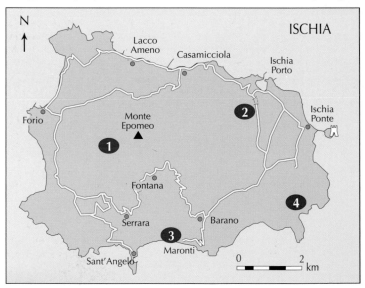

background, such as Cretaio, a corruption of 'crater', and Fango, from 'mud'. One of the most notable craters is now the main harbour, Ischia Porto. A 6th century BC eruption wiped out a Greek colony there and left a lake, later used for fish breeding, and in 1854 the King of Naples had it joined to the sea to make a sheltered port.

At other spots copious hot mineral springs are fed through spa resorts where guests are pampered, enjoying curative treatments such as mud baths, as the ancient Greeks and Romans did. The waters were long believed to be the hot tears of a repentant monstrous Titan, Typhon, imprisoned beneath Monte Epomeo as punishment by Zeus. For centuries he struggled underground, causing eruptions and earthquakes.

The volcanic heritage has blessed Ischia with divinely fertile soil; agriculture is widespread, with flourishing vineyards, citrus and vegetables galore.

Ischia is circled by an important road, the SS270, which serves all the key towns and resorts. On the southern reaches of the island it climbs in twists and turns to mountainside villages on the flanks of Monte Epomeo, the highest elevation. The northern coast has the main ports and good beaches, which continue along the eastern and southern extremities.

Ischia can only be reached by sea, with frequent ferries from both Naples (journey time 40–90min depending on type of service) and Sorrento, as well as Capri. See 'Getting There' in the main introduction for details of ferries. Ischia's main port is Ischia Porto, although ferries also come in to Casamicciola and Forio.

Visitors can bring their own cars over but it's hardly worth it because of the excellent low-cost public transport network, the tortuous mountain roads and holiday traffic jams. The buses are run by EAVBus (☎ 081 5429614) and the main terminal is at Ischia Porto. A three-day pass is €8 and timetables can be consulted at www.eavbus.it or www.ischiaonline.it. The most useful routes are CS or *circolare sinistra* (left circle) and CD, *circolare destra* (right circle), which circumnavigate the whole island. **Note** The waterfront village of Sant'Angelo is pedestrian-only and electric 'toy' taxis operate within its boundaries. The closest bus stop is Cava Grado.

Ischia has a real seaside feel about it with wonderful beaches. There is accommodation to suit all pockets. At Ischia Ponte the photogenic Mont-Saint-Michel-like promontory was fortified as the Castello Aragonese under Spanish rule in the 1400s, and people would take refuge there. Its monastery has been converted into a lovely hotel ☎ 081 992435 www.albergoil monastero.it.

At Ischia Porto there is the friendly waterfront Locanda sul Mare ☎ 081 981470 www.locanda sulmare.it, otherwise rooms are available c/o the shop L'Alveare

☎ 081 983420 mobile ☎ 368 669461. Quiet Sant'Angelo in the southwest of the island has many B&Bs as does the cliff-top Hotel Eugenio ☎ 081 993757 www.hoteleugenio.it. Not far away in the Olmitello valley off Lido dei Maronti is B&B Oasi La Vigna ☎ 081 990996 www.oasilavigna.it. There are camping grounds at Ischia Porto and Barano.

At the time of writing the main Tourist Office was at Casamicciola ☎ 081 5074231 www.infoischia procida.it.

The rock chapel of San Nicola, Monte Epomeo

WALK 1

Over Monte Epomeo

Walking time	3hr 15min
Difficulty	Grade 2
Ascent/Descent	327m/770m
Distance	9.3km/5.7 miles
Start/Finish	Fontana/Forio
Access	The mountainside village of Fontana on the SS270 road can be reached by CD or CS bus from Ischia Porto via all the main towns and villages.

At 787m Monte Epomeo is the island's highest peak, and one that regales spectacular views over the beautiful coast. Visible from all over the island, this landmark outcrop has a castle-like summit of so-called green tuff which has weathered into photogenic cavities. Not strictly a volcano, Monte Epomeo is the result of a powerful eruption that thrust pre-existing structures skyward, properly known as 'uplifted horst'. It occupies a surface area of 16km², approximately 34 per cent of the entire island.

In all probability the name Epomeo derives from ancient Greek for 'look around', an apt reference to its commanding position, but mythological accounts claim that it is one of the entrances to the underworld.

The walk descends through cool shady chestnut wood and vast expanses of ferns and broom to visit scattered rural settlements where fields are dotted with huge boulders. They detached themselves from the mountain during earthquakes and many have been transformed into troglodytic dwellings and stores. The route concludes at the attractive seaside town of Forio. In all, a memorable day's walk!

Overall the going is not especially difficult although the dearth of waymarks in the second half makes for

A superb and marvellously varied walk that crosses the mountainous western slice of Ischia climbing easily to Monte Epomeo and embracing a fascinating range of landscapes.

some uncertainty in terms of orientation. Take plenty of drinking water and sun protection. Fontana at the start has cafés and grocery stores, while en route refreshments and meals can be enjoyed at several places, such as on the actual mountaintop and at Santa Maria del Monte on the way down.

Drivers who prefer to limit their walk to Epomeo and return the same way can leave their vehicles at the car park above Fontana where the motorable road ends.

WALK

From the panoramic piazza at **Fontana** (460m), with its ochre-white church and Christ statue with outstretched arms, turn W along the main road in the direction of Serrara. Turn up the first steep surfaced lane R (signed for Epomeo). You join a wider surfaced road but soon leave it for an atmospheric sunken way through chestnut wood due N. The road is followed once more for a matter of metres to the **car park** and corner café-restaurant Grotto di Mezzavia (600m, 20min).

To the L of the buildings, a lovely lane climbs through beautiful chestnut wood. It narrows to a path cut into tuff then emerges on fern-covered slopes with stunning

Last leg to the summit

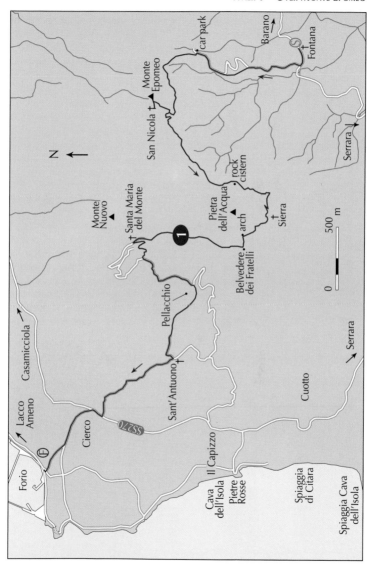

views. Steps lead across rock slopes, bearing R (NE) up via an inviting café terrace and eatery. Continue past the modest buildings but watch your step as it is a little exposed. Close by is the airy, amazing, wind-sculpted top of **Monte Epomeo** (787m, 40min). The spectacular outlook takes in Forio and Lacco Ameno at your feet and the spread of the island's north coast.

Backtracking, only metres below the summit lookout is the rock chapel of **San Nicola**, once home to a hermit. ◄ Return downhill below the café on the path followed earlier for 5min to a pair of iron gates – turn R on a white dirt lane in descent WSW flanked by bushy vegetation and masses of scented broom. Ignore the path turn-off R (an alternate shorter route for Santa Maria del Monte and Forio). Along the edge of a bowl-shaped depression, continue SW with brilliant views as far away as Vesuvius and the Monti Lattari on the mainland as well as Capri. A stretch S passes the prominent Pietra dell'Acqua outcrop and an ingenious old **rock cistern** with grooved channels for collecting water, essential for the crops grown up here. Between ferns, red valerian and brambles the rough lane loses height passing a couple of huts.

Keep your eyes peeled for a wooden arrow (for Santa Maria del Monte) where you turn off R (W). Soon

Adjacent but sadly out of bounds nowadays is a rock dwelling where a lone German soldier spent the war years.

Santa Maria del Monte

yellow paint dots lead between two huge rocks – keep R here. ▶ The broad gully NW drops through a wood of perfumed white-blossomed acacias below Pietra dell'Acqua. Wind down alongside a stretch of low old stone wall, keeping R at a junction. Despite the jumble of fallen rocks and overgrown stretches, the old stepped way is recognisable. An **arch** (520m) acts as an opening through a dry stone wall (which marks the intersection of the shorter variant from Epomeo, while L is a 'via panoramica' to Serrara.) Cut down through the trees W to reach **Belvedere dei Fratelli** (490m), the 'brothers' being three truncated stone pillars. The wonderful lookout takes in the sweep of Ischia's W coast, beyond a maze of roads and cultivated fields.

The detour L goes to Sierra with a cross and plaque in memory of RAF servicemen who lost their lives here in a 1947 plane crash.

Turn R (N) down a broad flight of steps that soon narrows to a scenic path cutting the western flank of Monte Epomeo. After a couple of huts is a pretty walled stretch on the edge of chestnut wood, a former hunting domain of the royal family from Naples. A modest but welcoming café/restaurant is encountered on the outskirts of **Santa Maria del Monte** (490m, 1hr 15min).

Turn sharp L (W) alongside the tiny domed church for a steep staircase and lane in gentler descent past houses. At a Christ statue ignore the ramp downhill and stick to the lane L (S), surfaced albeit rife with potholes. Below is a curious giant split boulder, its surface grooved by man-made water-collecting channels. You soon fork R on a concrete lane and realise that the rock has a house beneath it! This is **Pellacchio**. A rough path now tests knees as it plunges mostly NW down a cool gully, finally reaching another concrete lane. Ahead is a junction with a stone bench, only metres from a shrine to **Sant'Antuono**. On a quiet surfaced road now, turn R then immediately fork L as signed for Forio. Via Pulliero goes past rural properties adorned with jasmine and grapes. Down at **Cierco** on the main SS270 road, you can either catch a bus (stops for both directions are close by) or fork R then L for the final 10min to pretty waterfront Forio (10m, 1hr) which boasts a brilliant choice of beaches and *gelato* parlours.

WALK 2
Bosco della Maddalena

Walking time	1hr 45min
Difficulty	Grade 1–2
Ascent/Descent	300m/190m
Distance	5.5km/3.4 miles
Start/Finish	Parco Termale Castiglione bus stop/ Fiaiano
Access	On the main island road, the SS270, about halfway between Ischia Porto and Casamicciola is Castiglione and its spa where the walk starts. Principal bus lines including CS and CD come this way. From the village of Fiaiano where the walk finishes, bus No 6 loops back to Ischia Porto.

Starting out close to the island's north shore this interesting and little-visited route traverses to an inland village.

The going is straightforward on fairly clear paths and panoramic points are not lacking. En route an ancient volcano crater rim is visited; 350 metres across and 120 metres deep, it hosted a freshwater lake until 200–300 years ago. Rumour has it that the corpses of plague victims were cast into the crater in medieval times. The area is smothered in shady wood, a blend of Mediterranean plants and conifers. The latter were planted by the State Forestry Board (CFS, Corpo Forestale dello Stato) which manages the Bosco della Maddalena park traversed in the first part of the walk. It is equipped with handy map boards bearing bull's eye markers 'voi siete qui' (you are here) that facilitate orientation. Picnic tables abound though you may prefer local fare at the rustic trattoria or café at the low-key village of Fiaiano where the walk concludes.

WALK

From the Parco Termale Castiglione **bus stop** (20m) walk NW in the direction of Casamicciola. A matter of minutes

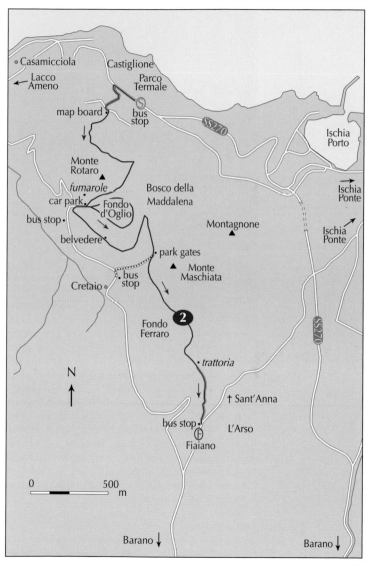

*The beautiful conifer
wood*

downhill, directly opposite the CFS office, a minor tarmac road (sign for *campo sportivo*) breaks off S. Wide curves go uphill through sweet-smelling pine wood. At the second bend fork L to the **map board** announcing the Bosco della Maddalena, then R (S) up the broad stepped way. This narrows to a path in steady ascent through holm oak and conifers, birdsong soon out-noising the hum of traffic. Bearing SE below Monte Rotaro another signboard is encountered, as are tiny cyclamens in the undergrowth. After a bench fork sharp R (SW) at the next junction and up to picnic tables. Here it's R again along the extant upper edge of the Fondo D'Oglio crater to a **car park** (220m, 30min) at a dead end road.

Now turn L below a concrete platform for the clear path gently uphill SE inside the long extinct volcano. Cutting the midriff of the crater, its S wall a sheer rock barrier, the route loops back to the **car park** (15min).

Cross the tarmac, though don't neglect to check out the group of nearby *fumarole* vents (R) that occasionally emit steam and heat the surrounding terrain. Follow the 'Belvedere Rotaro I' sign for the steps L (SW) and a fairly steep path up to the crest flanked by both aromatic flowering bushes and evergreens. A bench and board mark the site of the **belvedere** (307m). ▶ Continue E/NE around the top of the old crater to spots with excellent two-way views along with a clearer idea of the crater itself and its sunken centre, heavily wooded. When you finally reach a signboard and picnic area turn R (S) down a broad stepped way lined with pine trees. The wonderful outlook now ranges to the neighbouring island of Procida and even beyond Ischia to Vesuvius across the gulf. Through the **park gates** (240m, 35min), turn R along a shady lane.

In all likelihood the views will be obscured by trees, just allowing a glimpse of the tantalising sea!

Exit via Cretaio

An alternative exit continues W through to the village of Cretaio with café/restaurants and a bus back to Lacco Ameno on the north coast.

Not far along fork L (SSE) at a *trattoria* sign for the quiet road downhill. This follows the edge of another extinct volcano, the deep wooded pit of **Fondo Ferraro**.

Vast view from Fiaiano

To the left is the tiny white church of Sant'Anna and lovely pine wood that masks the island's youngest volcano, L'Arso, which last erupted in 1301.

At houses a path takes over with occasional waymarks in the shape of a lizard on a red background. Rural properties and old stone walls blooming with red valerian, serapias orchids, broom and ferns line the lovely way. After rustic **Trattoria La Cantina del Sargente** it's not far to the tarmac and glorious views to Ischia's landmark Castello Aragonese promontory E. Soon comes the main road through **Fiaiano** (170m, 25min) and a bus stop. ◄

WALK 3
Maronti to Sant'Angelo

Walking time	1hr 45min
Difficulty	Grade 1
Ascent/Descent	150m/165m
Distance	6.7km/4.2 miles
Start/Finish	Lido dei Maronti /Cava Grado (the bus stop for Sant'Angelo)
Access	Forking south from the township of Barano a minor road descends in wide curves to the seafront Lido dei Maronti. Buses No 5 and No 11 come here. At the walk end, Cava Grado is served by lines No 1, CS and CD to all major localities. Additional transport is available during the walk thanks to the water taxis that ferry passengers between the beach and Sant'Angelo.

On the island's southernmost coast this is a gorgeous walk along a great beach of volcanic sand with inviting spreads of deckchairs.

The name Lido dei Maronti may be a reference to the erstwhile presence of a Maronite community. The beautiful sweep of bay extends west from Punta della Signora, one of the few accessible sections of this coast as it lacks the usual forbidding cliffs. En route two curious canyons sculpted from the friable earth by rivulets are explored. The first is atmospheric Olmitello, named after a type of elm.

The second, known as Cavascura, has a spa, now low-key yet of great historic importance. It was especially well known to ancient populations who appreciated the curative properties of its mineral-rich waters for treating rheumatism and respiration and miraculously reversing the effects of ageing! The name derives from Greek for 'extreme heat', referring to the 70°C spring water that bubbles out of the ground. In Roman times it reportedly boasted magnificent altars and small temples. The great orator Cicero wrote of the beach 'where beneath the sand and the sea floor burns the heart of a volcano and in the valley of Cavascura flows boiling hot water'. Then in the 14th century a physician at the Spanish court wrote of the spa as a 'fountainhead of health and youth and useful for all limb pain and digestion'. Here from April to October (www.cavascura.it) modern-day visitors can give it a go, at 'worst' indulging in a relaxing thermal bath or sauna in premises dug directly out of the hillside. All around are bizarre shapes, earth pyramids and 'organ pipes' created by ongoing atmospheric erosion.

To top it off, a bonus volcano-related phenomenon at the far end of the beach is the collection of steaming

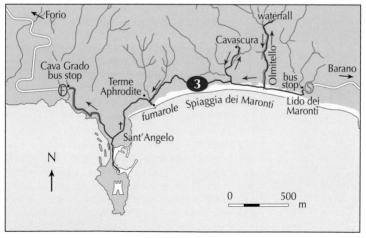

The walk in Cavascura

fumarole, from the Latin for 'smoke'. Don't get too close as temperatures reach a burning 100°C. Hot sand baths and warm water swims are the order of the day here, though people also take advantage of the free energy to cook food by simply burying it on the beach! Clearly the walk can be stretched out to a relaxing day.

Near the end of the walk is the pretty fishing hamlet of Sant'Angelo with its photogenic port and promontory and its maze of car-free alleyways and flights of stairs. You're spoilt for choice with clusters of cafés and restaurants, as well as hotels – see the Ischia introduction for ideas.

WALK
From the bus stop at **Lido dei Maronti** (15m) go down to the beach itself and turn R (W) across the darkish sand past the string of inviting cafés. A short stroll away is the fork R (N) for **Olmitello**, a stream valley cut deep into the soft terrain. Past a tiny hotel then a shady café-cum-guesthouse, a path proceeds inland beneath fascinating eroded flanks with elongated mushrooms of fragile rock topped with precarious stones. After a ruined building and a somewhat grotty *sorgente* (spring), continue past

a small dam. Here you are dwarfed by taller cliffs colonised by tree spurge and broom to where the valley forks. Flow permitting, the R fork can be followed as far as is safe. However the wider L part with arches and rock towers is more impressive. The winding canyon resulting from flowing water is marvellously atmospheric and can be followed as far as a modest **waterfall**. Return to the seafront afterwards (45min).

Resume the sandy walking under light grey cliffs to the nearby turn-off for **Cavascura** and what's left of the ancient spa. The entrance is a short way in; a modest entrance fee is charged.

Head back towards the sea. ▶ Just before the seafront and a hotel turn R up a steep lane through a tunnel to a scenic paved stretch, marginally inland. Caper plants straggle down the hillsides. Past houses and gardens further ahead this descends to more *terme* (spas) spouting steam. Branch L to the nearby Spiaggia di Grado (25min) to see the **fumarole** in the sand, but keep your distance!

Backtrack then continue on the L fork uphill past **Terme Aphrodite** amid the pong of sulphur fumes. This high path affords divine bay views. Follow signs L for

If you opt for sand and a swim, ignore the following instructions and rejoin the walk at the fumarole.

Sant'Angelo backed by Monte Epomeo

47

'*centro*' past the church of San Michele, and soon branch L down to the pretty fishing port lined by whitewashed houses and waterfront cafés of **Sant'Angelo** (0m, 20min). High above looms Monte Epomeo.

After a wander around this charming spot you need the way NNW over grey cliffs around the next bay via the car park to the **Cava Grado bus stop** (30m, 15min).

WALK 4
Piano Liguori Traverse

Walking time	2hr
Difficulty	Grade 2
Ascent/Descent	230m/270m
Distance	5.3km/3.3 miles
Start/Finish	Campagnano/Molara
Access	From Ischia Porto buses No 8 and C12 serve Campagnano, a short but tortuous detour off the main island road. Molara at the end is on the busy SS270 a short distance from Pilastri, and is served by lines CD and CS amongst others.

A worthwhile little-frequented route around the southeastern corner of the island affording vast views over the Gulf of Naples to Vesuvius and the Sorrento peninsula.

Here steep terraced hillsides are traversed, where grapes and crops have been cultivated for generations. Well away from the glamour of the spa resorts and beaches, the route provides insights into traditional island life where man and mule worked side by side in the fields, though the occasional trail bike and even motorised wheelbarrows have recently found their way down the lanes.

The halfway mark, Piano Liguori, is a tiny hamlet with just a handful of inhabitants who trudge up a steep lane from the nearest road head carrying their shopping. One enterprising soul runs a rustic eatery mostly

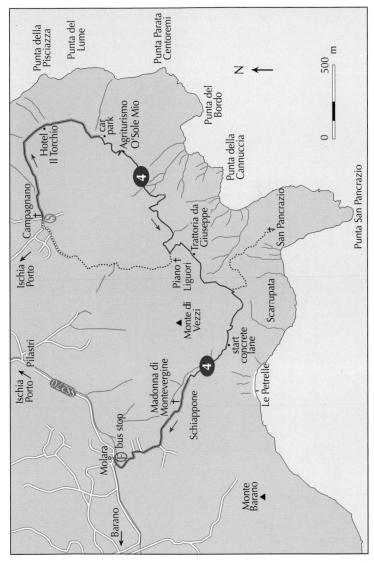

49

for foreign walkers; a simple lunch and a glass of local wine can be enjoyed along with great coast views. A second lunch spot, closer to the start, is Agriturismo O'Sole Mio. Otherwise picnic supplies can be purchased at Campagnano where the walk starts.

Be aware that the route is not always obvious and landmarks are few and far between, so directions need to be followed carefully and allowances made for wrong turns. Special care is recommended at several exposed and potentially slippery bits towards the end. Bear in mind that the terrain in this part of the world is friable and prone to slides during wet conditions. The opposite also holds true – dust prevails in protracted hot weather.

The route can be shortened by exiting halfway and returning to Campagnano on the old mule track, shorter, straightforward and less panoramic than the main path. Alternately a rewarding but tiring steep extension visits the chapel of San Pancrazio on its eponymous headland below Piano Liguori – allow at least 1hr 30min extra for the return detour. See below for details of where to turn off the main path.

The Castello Aragonese and Ischia Ponte

WALK

Start in the piazza of **Campagnano** (170m) with its 18th-century Chiesa d'Annunziata, the facade sporting weather-worn ceramics under twin bell towers. Take Via Campagnano, the narrow road R of the church, downhill E through rural properties. Lovely views can be enjoyed to the Castello Aragonese on its headland. A gentle uphill stretch sees you rounding a scenic point with pastel houses looking to the neighbouring island of Procida and beyond to the mainland and Vesuvius, if you're lucky. Bearing S past **Hotel Il Torchio** and elegant pink Palazzo Quartaruolo, the road narrows a little. Still surfaced, it climbs steadily past modest houses and gardens. Soon after a panoramic point with a pine tree and **car park** (30min) is a strategic fork – keep L (SW) as per red arrows for the '*agriturismo*'. A dusty path and more paint sploshes lead past **Agriturismo O'Sole Mio**. Vineyards and gullies are traversed on the ensuing level stretch high above the rugged coast. ▶ A wooden handrail and retaining walls of dark volcanic stone run along the way, and the odd bench is encountered, as well as pockets of holm oak and wild flowers in sheltered spots.

The vast outlook extends to the Sorrento peninsula and the Monti Lattari, as well as Capri, visibility permitting.

About 20min along, at a large sign for 'Piano Liguori' turn R up a shallow clay gully overhung with tall grasses and occasionally overgrown. This proceeds NW for the most part. A handrail and signs point you up to a shady sunken way past ruined stone buildings and fenced-in fields where artichokes, lemons and grapes thrive. Power poles appear, then an intersection with a bench and map is reached at **Piano Liguori** (340m, 30min), where paved lanes radiate in various directions.

Exit to Campagnano (30min)
Straight on is a cross marking the turn-off R (N) for a clear well-trodden lane through fields and woodland. It becomes a surfaced road for the final stretch NE past blocks of flats, leading back to the square and bus stop of **Campagnano** (170m) where the walk started.

Turn sharp L (SE) downhill through a village-scape belonging to the 1950s. Tiny stone houses and flights of steps serve the few remaining inhabitants, one of whom runs the modest **Trattoria da Giuseppe** with a peaceful terrace that enjoys wonderful views over the Gulf of Naples.

Going R from here, the narrow but clear path curves SW through gardens, with a magnificent outlook, and skirts over an awesome eroded gully. Far below is the prominent headland of Punta San Pancrazio. Not far on, just as the path begins to descend steeply on tiny steps (which lead to the chapel of San Pancrazio far below, a 1hr 30min strenuous detour), leave it by forking R. This leads to a level stretch with infrequent red paint markings. It curves up past a modest house and power pole, bearing WSW on a rugged headland high above the dramatic Scarrupata cliffs. Nearby around a point is a narrow tricky tract hugging a fence – watch your step! Views are spectacular, to Le Petrelle pebble beach and sweep of bay below Monte Barano as well as Monte Epomeo beyond. On an old path excavated out of light volcanic terrain you plunge W towards a house with a green roof. Broom bushes and masses of serapias orchids line the way, and modest Monte di Vezzi comes into view N. Steps appear, then a **concrete lane** which conducts walkers away from the coast and inland past houses and chestnut wood. At a fork dominated by overhanging tree roots keep L through peaceful countryside. Only minutes on is 14th-century church Madonna di Montevergine at **Schiappone**. Steep tarmac continues NW in descent to a metal cross where you bear R for the last leg through to the main road SS270, shops and bus stop at **Molara** (119m, 1hr).

Steep steps and dramatic views on the last leg

CAPRI

The Faro

INTRODUCTION

> *The island of Capri consists of little else than a picturesque and rugged mass of rock standing in the sea, of stern and forbidding aspect... The wild and precipitous cliffs remind one of Norway; the village reminds one of Egypt and Syria; the patches of luxuriant vegetation in the midst of rugged rocks remind one of the Isles of Greece; and yet Capri is unlike all other places – it is Capri.*
> Cook's Handbook to Southern Italy (1905)

It's easy to understand why the Roman Emperors made this gem of an island their playground, taking time out from the hectic affairs of the capital to build 12 grandiose imperial villas. Capri is picture-postcard perfect, with breathtaking scenery every way you look: soaring cliffs of limestone where raucous colonies of seagulls perch, overlooking turquoise coves; gay pastel-stuccoed houses amid well-tended gardens overflowing with luxuriant plants; and off-the-chart luxury hotels catering for international glitterati and the well-heeled who have been flocking here for centuries.

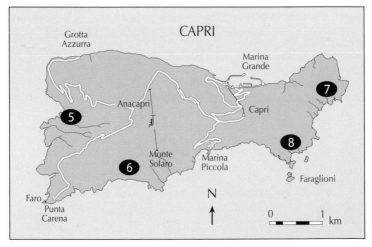

Legend has it the island of Capri was once a beautiful nymph. As is the nature of mankind, she was the object of the obsessive desire and longing of youthful Vesuvius. As his unwanted attentions heated up he lunged at her. She backed off and leapt into the sea to turn into an island, far from his reach but in clear view. This sent him crazy and his sighs were fiery. So Vesuvius in turn transformed himself into rock, a volcano, looming over the city of Naples, which has suffered terribly from his burning rage and trembling ever since.

Measuring a mere 6km in length and 2.8km at its widest point, Capri covers 10km^2 and has 17km of coastline. Be aware that the appellation Capri is used for the island as a whole as well as the main albeit modest town occupying the eastern part. With its network of narrow paved lanes and stepped alleys this sector is blessedly car-free. To replace the mules once used for transport, clean battery-powered trolleys trundle around loaded high with supplies and luggage. The central focus is Piazza Umberto I, a charmingly elegant square with a miniature bell tower. It is chock-full of inviting cafés, bustling waiters and hedonistic tourists VIP-spotting, and never seems to sleep. This is the start for easy walks to unmissable island sights such as the awesome Arco Naturale, Faraglioni stacks and a Roman villa.

In the west is Anacapri on its elevated stone platform, surrounded by cultivated fields and a clutch of country villas. All is dominated by Monte Solaro, the island's highest point and a lookout par excellence. For centuries access to Anacapri was by the so-called 'Scala Fenicia' (Phoenician staircase) cut into the rock face by the ancient Greeks, and still usable. The road around the precipitous mountainside was not built until 1877, and the two towns continue to lead surprisingly separate existences with an ongoing sense of rivalry. The routes described on this western side of the island are little trodden, and solitary at times.

Generally speaking, despite the astronomically high tourist numbers – visitors seem to outnumber the locals – most day-trippers to Capri concentrate at a couple of hot spots. Things quieten down considerably of an evening when the groups return to the mainland or to cruise ships moored off Sorrento.

Unless you splash out on a helicopter, you'll need to take a ferry to reach Capri. Fast and slow ships depart from Naples (40min and 50min respectively), Sorrento (20min or 40min), Ischia, as well as the Amalfi Coast in season – see 'Getting There' in the main introduction. The sheltered harbour is at Marina Grande, one of the few places where cliffs don't prevent easy access to the sea. Visitors glide up to the town on the *funiculare*, otherwise it's a 20min uphill stroll. Small orange ATC buses (☎ 081 8370420) zip along

Villa Jovis is surrounded by trees

the narrow roads connecting the port with Capri and Anacapri; Staiano Trasporti (☎ 081 8372422) is responsible for the runs beyond Anacapri to the Faro and Grotta Azzurra. Timetables can be consulted at www.capritourism.com, including the Monte Solaro chair lift (*seggiovia*). Do invest in a multi-day transport pass for anything more than a single day's visit.

Prices for everything on Capri are noticeably higher than elsewhere, but it's worth shelling out to stay a couple of days here and drink in the beauty. (It might be the only sort of imbibing you can afford!) Here are some (not exactly budget) suggestions from the vast range of accommodation possibilities: centrally located Stella Maris ☎ 081 8370452 albergostellamaris@libero.it and peaceful Pensione La Tosca ☎ 0818370989 www.latoscahotel.com. Slightly cheaper options may be found at Anacapri. Tourist Information Offices can be found at the port and in Capri itself ☎ 081 8370686 www.capritourism.com.

WALK 5
Sentiero dei Fortini

Walking time	2hr 30min
Difficulty	Grade 2
Ascent/Descent	65m/140m
Distance	5km/3.1 miles
Start/Finish	Faro/Grotta Azzurra
Access	Both the Faro and Grotta Azzurra are linked by bus to Anacapri, whence Capri *centro*.

Peaceful and solitary, this walk traverses a veritable garden of herbs and unusual Mediterranean plants. Along the path artistic ceramic 'books' with interesting details of the local flora and fauna, in both Italian and English, are set on rocks. The cliffs here are lower than the other awesome edges of the island, and thus in the past more vulnerable to attack. The coast is dotted with

The 'Sentiero dei Fortini' (path of the forts) is a gorgeous new route running along the beautiful western coast of Capri.

The inviting cove near the walk's start

photogenic forts dating back to the early 1800s, when the Napoleonic wars were in full swing and Capri was strategic in terms of sea access and supply routes. Sworn rivals, the British and French took turns in seizing the island. Both were responsible for erecting the military constructions, naturally in spots with wonderful views of both sea and land.

The path is accessible to walkers of all abilities and experience. Numerous flights of steps are encountered but all are in good condition and have reasonable gradients.

Of extra interest, the Faro or lighthouse near the start is the second largest in Italy, after that at Genoa. It and its old fort can be admired at close quarters after a short detour SW from the bus stop to Punta Carena before embarking on the walk. A tempting dip in the inviting turquoise cove only metres below is an excuse for further delay, though rest assured that en route is a string of rocky inlets for memorable swims. Lastly, a lovely spot to 'chill out' if the day's hot, or to enjoy a simple lunch on the terrace, is the snack bar a little over halfway. There's nothing else until the very end. Otherwise purchase picnic supplies beforehand, and bring plenty of drinking water and sunscreen.

Several exit routes for Anacapri are encountered; most lead up to the road and bus stops. At the walk's conclusion is the Grotta Azzurra, one of Capri's greatest tourist magnets. Visitors are rowed in small craft through the low cave entrance. When the official opening hours are over, audacious swimmers can go in alone, however waves can make it dangerous.

WALK

From the **Faro** bus stop (40m) go down the steps then R to the official start of the 'Sentiero dei Fortini' and the first of the informative ceramic plaques. The broad path climbs gently NNE on graded stone steps through the sweet-smelling *pineta* (pine wood) of Limmo, with glimpses of Torre della Guardia perched on a high cliff overhead. The road is touched on briefly where Walk 6 from Monte Solaro arrives and a good path continues parallel to the tarmac. Go down a concrete ramp to a detour L leading

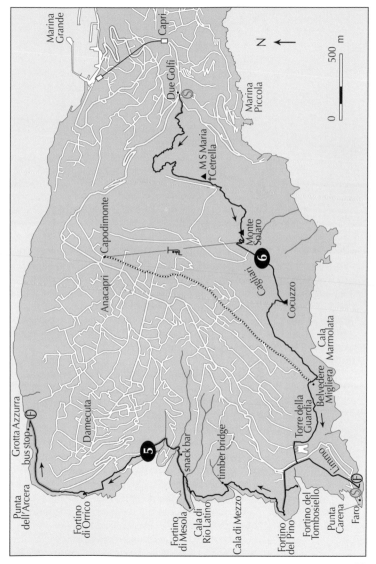

Fortino del Tombosiello and the Faro

The small cannon here, known as a carronade, dates back to 1808 but was only brought out of its watery resting place in 2000, found by fishermen after heavy storms. It had been cast into the sea by the British in the face of French attack.

to **Fortino del Tombosiello** overlooking a cove of the same name. ◄

In descent resume the ramp which concludes at **Fortino del Pino**, the largest of the forts and a good spot for fossils. Now brace yourself for the most beautiful part, dropping along a breathtaking stretch of limestone rock eroded by wind and water. While not that high above the sea it does come close to the edge and can feel a little exposed so take your time. It's a veritable botanical garden dominated by pungent everlasting with its felty-yellow blooms. A few ups and downs lead essentially N. After a rise the path drops to round a mini fjord inlet Cala di Mezzo traversed on a **timber bridge**.

Over artistic weather-sculpted rocks dotted with flowers and fishermen, a house is reached (signed exit for Anacapri) then it's down to a rock platform. Here a flight of rock steps drop to the deep blue waters of **Cala di Rio Latino** for the joy of swimmers. Otherwise keep R past the ruins of a lime kiln (*calcara*) then head inland (NE) past another exit path for Anacapri. Soon fork L for the stretch to imposing **Fortino di Mesola** (1hr 20min) on Punta Campetiello.

Back at the fork on the main path continue E through shady vegetation. Inviting signs urge you on to the friendly **snack bar** just around the corner. Afterwards, the path dips through holm oak for a stony path climbing on Passo della Capra, dry stony terrain and a cliff colonised by colourful tree spurge. Properties obscure coast views but not for long. (Ignore the two forks R for 'Grotta Azzurra' unless you wish to reach the road.) Veer L as soon as possible back down to water views and **Fortino di Orrico** (45min) on its rocky perch. The fort was the stage for a landmark 1808 battle when the French took it back from the British, regaining control of the island. It boasts a lovely outlook S taking in the other forts, as well as the distant island of Ischia NW, visibility permitting. Moreover dolphins and even whale sightings are reported here. High above rises the Damecuta headland, home to a Roman villa and birds of prey.

Due N now an area of windswept bushes and trees is encountered as you approach the road near Punta dell'Arcera, named after woodcock, as netting birds was once practised here. Go L (E) along the narrow tarmac way to the walk's conclusion at the **Grotta Azzurra bus stop** (35m, 25min), a short flight of steps away from the world-famous cave; a restaurant, café and baths are also at hand.

The walk's breathtaking central stretch

WALK 6

Over Monte Solaro

Walking time	3hr 30min
Difficulty	Grade 3
Ascent/Descent	460m/560m
Distance	6km/3.7 miles
Start/Finish	Due Golfi/Faro
Access	Due Golfi is the busy intersection between the roads from the Marina Grande port, Anacapri and Capri township. It is easily reached by ATC bus from all directions. On foot from the centre of Capri and the upper funicular station allow 10min. The Faro at walk's end has frequent buses to Anacapri where you change for Capri.

An extended traverse from Capri township over the mountain to the island's southwestern corner.

A spectacular and adventurous route far away from it all on this otherwise tourist-ridden island. The opening section follows the Sentiero del Passetiello, the route used to link Capri with Anacapri on its mountainous platform prior to the construction of the motorable road. A strenuous climb is entailed through wood and flowered slopes, as is a little scrambling during the ascent to Monte Solaro (589m). This is the highest point on Capri and a popular lookout thanks to a chair lift – handy for accessing/exiting the walk. The ensuing path negotiates a breathtaking – not to mention exposed – razor sharp cliff top ridge via a string of belvederes en route to the landmark Faro lighthouse on Punta Carena, the conclusion.

Don't underrate the length or difficulty and wear shoes with a good grip. Long trousers are probably a good idea too as overgrown stretches can mean scratchy vegetation. The walk is unsuitable for anyone who has a problem with heights and it is important to remember that bad weather and strong winds can make it dangerous. Allow a whole day as you'll be taking lots of time out for photos, bird watching and a well-earned swim at the end. Take plenty of drinking water and sun screen and a picnic unless you plan on lunching at Monte Solaro. Time and energy permitting, a brilliant 2hr extension is possible by slotting into the Sentiero dei Fortini just before the Faro – see Walk 5.

This route is easily split into two completely separate walks hinging on Monte Solaro, thanks to the year-round daily chair lift link with Capodimonte at Anacapri. In addition, an easy 1hr 30min walk can be done by starting out at Capodimonte. Take the pedestrian Via Caposcuro S past the church Santa Maria a Costantinopoli. The street becomes Via Migliera and leads in gentle ascent SW out of the built-up district through veggie plots to Belvedere Migliera. Whence the main route to Faro for a return to Anacapri by bus.

The walk starts at Due Golfi which, as the name suggests, looks to the sea on both sides of Capri. The locals used to set up nets here to catch quails on their twice-yearly migrations. This was an important economic activity and the island's bishop himself derived a large part of his income from hunting duties.

WALK

At the **Due Golfi** intersection (140m), turn down Via Marina Piccola. Just after the entrance to the Ospedale take the pedestrian alley R, signed by a ceramic plaque for 'Sentiero del Passetiello'. Due W at first it heads towards a forbidding limestone barrier. A stepped way with ramps climbs past houses and vegetable gardens, following signs at forks.

After about 15min a red arrow points R (N) onto a clear path in shady holm oak and pine wood dotted with oyster plants. Mostly level, it passes under cliffs to a marked fork where you go L, decidedly uphill. This climbs to rock steps where a hands-on clamber gets you through a narrow cleft. ▶

All effort is amply rewarded as you emerge at a stunningly scenic spot: Marina Piccola and the Faraglioni rock stacks are at your feet, while back east is Capri town.

The narrow path continues up the steep mountain slope carpeted with rock roses and silver bush, seagulls wheeling around the sheer crags close at hand. The ridge top is gained and crossed and the path bears S high over a quiet green valley. Thick broom bushes are encountered along with asphodels and wild gladioli. Soon after modest **Monte Santa Maria** (495m) is the beautifully located tiny 14th-century Eremo di Santa Maria at **Cetrella** (1hr 30min), sporadically open to visitors. The name may derive from *erba cedrina* or lemon balm which grows here. ◀ Looming SW now is Monte Solaro, its summit protected by pine trees.

In 1930. Norman Douglas described Citrella as 'poised like a swallow's nest upon its windswept limestone crag'.

A broad track leads off R (NW) – ignore it for the enjoyable path. From the church gate take the faint path L to reach the nearby *rotonda* lookout. Then at an old house keep L past the terrace for the clear path marked with frequent red paint splashes. Bearing SW–W it makes its spectacular way through low vegetation over dizzy cliff edges.

Monte Solaro (589m, 20min), the highest point on Capri, is easily gained. A popular spot with visitors who ride the chair lift from Anacapri, and a handy exit point

Fantastic views from Monte Solaro

for those who decide to conclude the walk at this point.
As well as enjoying the café and restaurant, here you can
drink in the marvellous 360° spectacle over the whole
island, as well as the Monti Lattari and Sorrento peninsula, and far beyond to Naples and Vesuvius, not forgetting the stomach-churning drop down the Ventroso to the
sea.

When you're ready to move on, go down to the
departure point for the chair lift, where you need the path
that leads under the cables (ask the operator if needs be).
Past a concentration of orchids it quickly turns L (SW) to
negotiate a razor sharp ridge – on its land side, thankfully, high over the Cagliari woodland. Apart from occasional exposure, the path's good and has frequent red
paint splashes. ▶ After the rocky pointof **Cocuzzo** (495m)
the path zigzags decidedly in descent, still following the
ridge. Pine wood spells welcome shade for a while. As
you reach a building, follow the wire fence to Belvedere
dei Filosofi with its rusty cross, a magnificent spot high
over Cala Marmolata. ▶

A concrete-based path proceeds past a Madonna
statue to wonderful **Belvedere Migliera** (300m, 1hr), fitted with comfortable benches.

Amazing views
and seagulls, rock
roses and scented
broom are constant
companions.

The landmark
lighthouse (Faro) is
now visible beyond
rugged eroded
outcrops.

Exit to Capodimonte (40min)

From here a lane, Via Migliera, leads inland NE through scattered homes and
vegetable plots, bearing N into the residential area of Anacapri. Becoming
Via Caposcuro it concludes at the chair lift departure station at Capodimonte
(285m), close to a bus stop.

Follow the path W marked with red paint splashes.
After a house a fence is followed along the edge of prop-
erties not far from a distinctive watchtower, **Torre della
Guardia**. A dog-leg R takes you through to a surfaced lane,
where you go L. Soon after the first bend a path breaks off
L, signed for Faro. Steep steps fitted with a handrail plunge
W past agaves and cypress trees to the road. Cross over
to the other side and, unless you wish to embark on the

beautiful 'Sentiero dei Fortini' track (Walk 5), turn L on the broad way for the final 20min. Through the scented pine copse of Limmo this brings you out onto a concrete walkway where you turn L up the steps for the **Faro** bus stop (40m, 40min). The monumental lighthouse, the second largest in Italy after Genoa, is only minutes away out on Punta Carena alongside an old fort. However, downhill you can also enjoy a well-deserved swim off the rocks in the beautiful cove below, or use the facilities of the bathing establishment, complete with café.

WALK 7
Villa Jovis Loop

Walking time	2hr
Difficulty	Grade 1–2
Ascent/Descent	160m/160m
Distance	5.5km/3.4 miles
Start/Finish	Piazza Umberto I, Capri *centro*
Access	From the Marina Grande, the town square and walk start can be reached by either a short ATC bus ride or the funicular railway. Otherwise allow a pleasant 20min uphill on foot.

This superb unforgettable walk heads out of the centre of Capri town and along pretty paved lanes past elegant villas and gardens.

The destination is the divine promontory of Monte Tiberio occupied by Villa Jovis, the brainchild of the 1st-century AD Roman Emperor Tiberius. The vast sprawling complex stands mostly in ruins nowadays, but it is remarkably evocative. It doubles as a belvedere extraordinaire with views towards the Punta Campanella tip of the Monti Lattari-Sorrento peninsula, without forgetting the immense sweep of the gulf where Vesuvius broods over Naples in the distance.

Afterwards a pretty path drops around Capri's northeastern point via an art deco villa, Villa Fersen.

Inside Villa Jovis

An intriguing contrast to Villa Jovis, it dates back to 1905 when it was designed for dandy Jacques Fersen D'Adelsward at the height of Capri's fame and fashion. Fitted with marble staircases, swish bathrooms and a garden temple, it also boasted an opium den, where the owner apparently died from an overdose of cocaine.

Afterwards you amble back into town.

All the 'roads' followed today are pedestrian-only lanes, alleys or paths with plentiful ceramic signs pointing the way. A handful of cafés and restaurants is encountered en route, otherwise should you prefer to be independent take a picnic – groceries and ready-made sandwiches are easily purchased in town.

Allow plenty of extra time for visits: Villa Jovis is open daily from 9am to an hour before sunset; Villa Fersen from 10am–1pm/2–5pm, closed Sun.

WALK

In bustling **Piazza Umberto I** (150m) to the L of the Municipio building, a gorgeous red bougainvillea vine marks the entrance to a covered passageway. This is Via Longoni, the name a derivation from the Greek for 'long

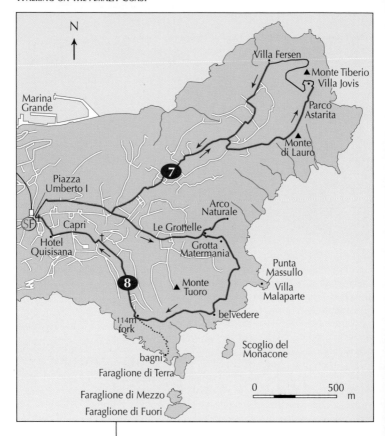

stones', as it follows 8th-century BC megalithic walls. Take this narrow alleyway N lined with shops, then at a dead end go R (E) onto Via Sopramonte, at a corner house where Lenin was a guest in 1910. It's not far to an intersection with a café and small supermarket where you fork uphill L (NE) on Via Tiberio. This climbs gently past beautifully tended gardens, residential villas and a school, then as buildings become scarcer, vegetable plots and towering Maritime Pine trees are the norm. After the turn-off for Via Lo Capo and the return loop, ignored for the time being, a brief stretch S with a steeper gradient sees you on Via Maiuri close to Monte di Lauro. You soon flank the low stone walls of wooded **Parco Astarita**; should you be lucky and find it open, duck in for the great views. Only minutes away is the entrance to **Villa Jovis** (335m, 50min), one of Capri's 12 imperial villas dedicated to divinities, this one for *Giove*, Italian for Jupiter.

Alongside the ticket office are awesome plunging sea views and the so-called 'Salto di Tiberio', a 200m-high cliff where the cruel emperor reputedly had insubordinate servants – along with undesired guests – cast to their death on the jagged rocks below. The villa premises were excavated systematically in the 1930s, and total 5500 square metres on different levels. Surrounded by shady pine trees and scented Mediterranean shrubs, it is a warren of rooms and arched passageways to baths and massive cisterns for collecting precious rainwater. Upper level terraces and a church on the edge of vertical limestone cliffs where wheeling seagulls and birds of prey nest, double as brilliant lookouts. ▸

With Punta Campanella relatively close to the north across the water, it is easy to understand that Capri was a progression of the limestone Monti Lattari.

Villa Fersen

69

Back at the entrance to Villa Jovis, turn R (NW) on a new path through woods of holm oak and attractive dwarf palms. It circles beneath the archaeological site before launching down steep steps accompanied by pretty rock roses and beautiful sea views. It's not far to **Villa Fersen** (230m, 20min), another divine if melancholic spot.

Resume the walk by taking Via Lo Capo SW through woodland and gardens. At a T-junction go L – this leads back to Via Tiberio. Now retrace the route taken on the outward stretch, following signs for 'Capri Centro' back to **Piazza Umberto I** (150m, 50min).

WALK 8
Arco Naturale–Faraglioni Circuit

Walking time	1hr 45min
Difficulty	Grade 1–2
Ascent/Descent	120m/120m
Distance	4km/2.5 miles
Start/Finish	Piazza Umberto I, Capri *centro*
Access	See Walk 7

For route map, see Walk 7.

A beautiful, scenic walk by anyone's standards!

This walk circles the island's southeastern extremity via a clutch of brilliant must-see highlights: the breathtaking Arco Naturale and the three spectacular world-famous Faraglioni rock stacks that shoot skywards out of the turquoise sea. One of these splendid 'beacons', the Faraglione di Fuori, is home to a rare metallic blue lizard *Lacerta viridens faraglionensis*, found nowhere else in the world; its bright colouring is believed to be a technique for blending in with its surrounds unless designed to repulse the noisy voracious seagulls who dwell nearby! Lastly, a neighbouring pinnacle, Scoglio del Monacone, is reputedly the burial site for Masgaba, the highly respected African architect of Emperor Ottaviano Augusto. It takes

The awesome Arco Naturale

its name from either the Mediterranean monk seal which once swam in these waters, or a local hermit monk.

Paths are clear and mostly paved, the only slight drawback being the steep steps encountered in descent, around halfway. While not technically difficult, there are 270 of them, all knee testing. Just before they begin near the Arco Naturale, an atmospheric under-the-cliffs café-eatery (Bar Trattoria Le Grottelle ☎ 081 8375719) offers a lovely terrace for meditation and charging your batteries.

WALK

In bustling **Piazza Umberto I** (150m) to the L of the Municipio building, a gorgeous red bougainvillea vine marks the entrance to a covered passageway. This is Via Longoni, the name a derivation from the Greek for 'long stones', as it follows 8th-century BC megalithic walls. Take this narrow alleyway N lined with shops, then at a dead end go R (E) onto Via Sopramonte, at a corner house where Lenin sojourned in 1910. It's not far to an intersection with a café and small supermarket where you bear R (SE) on Via Matermania. This continues at an

71

easy pace through an elegant residential area and glorious well-loved gardens overflowing with exotic species. At a roadside shrine keep L (E) at two successive forks as signed for 'Arco Naturale'. Soon, close to a limestone cliff face is welcoming **Bar Trattoria Le Grottelle**, a lovely spot for a drink or meal.

Take the L fork down steps to the nearby amazing **Arco Naturale** (200m, 30min). Rising from dense greenery, the dramatic limestone arch cannot fail to elicit 'oohs' and 'aahs' from even the most sightseed tourist. The eroded keyhole, once the entrance to a long-collapsed cavern, is a window onto the turquoise sea hundreds of metres below. Once you've had your fill and taken dozens of near-identical photos, return to **Le Grottelle** and take the L fork now for Via Pizzolungo. This is the beginning of the 'infamous' stone staircase, due E at first to the awesome rock overhang hosting **Grotta Matermania**. Dedicated to the 'God mother' or *Cibele*, the vast grotto was transformed during Roman times into a nymphaeum with a gushing spring, the cavern consolidated with brick walls decorated with glass mosaics and shells.

The stepped path continues SSE in unremitting descent through shady holm oak wood alive with birdsong, and offers tantalising glimpses of the gorgeous sea and limestone cliffs. Not far along on Punta Massullo stands spectacular three-storey Villa Malaparte with its salmon-stuccoed facade and to-die-for roof terrace.

Cutting across limestone flanks dotted with pine, lentisc and pink domes of tree spurge, Via Pizzolungo now (thankfully) becomes a gentle stroll SW, simply beautiful. And soon you get your first sight of the majestic Faraglioni, justifiably must-sees, best admired from the nearby **belvedere**. Towering jagged stacks, they soar 100 metres out of the sea, dwarfing the tiny boats that duck and bob at their base.

Continue W past a white house for a fork L and a short but worthwhile detour to yet another lookout in the shade of elegant Maritime Pines. Back on the main path beneath Monte Tuoro you proceed past houses and carob trees to a **114m fork**.

Capri's magnificent Faraglioni

Descent to the sea
Here an optional 300m stepped descent means access to the Faraglioni
bagni where you can swim off the rocks or make use of bathing facilities and
cafés (allow 30min return).

Proceeding NNW soon the vast sweep of the island's
southern coast, including Marina Piccola and Monte
Solaro, can be admired. Now Via Tragara leads easily past
renowned Hotel Punta Tragara and through a succession
of luxury villas and gardens amid a marvellous celebra-
tion of scents and colours. Some contrast to the area's
name, which is derived from the Greek for 'goat pen'!

At the junction with the German church the way
bears W as Via Camerette, its uphill side a procession of
boutiques opposite a line-up of olive and palm trees. At
magnificent **Hotel Quisisana** turn R up a shop-crammed
street and back to **Piazza Umberto I** (150m, 1hr 15min).

SORRENTO

Admiring the legendary Grotte delle Sirene (Walk 12)

INTRODUCTION

Hummed the world over, the second most famous Neapolitan song (after O' Sole Mio), 'Torna a Surriento' – 'Come Back to Sorrento' – exhorted a leading Italian politician in 1902 to return with funds desperately needed for repairing roads and dilapidated buildings. Tourism undoubtedly contributed to bringing about the desired result. A key stop for Grand Tourers in the 1800s, the attractive old town of Sorrento boasts a spectacular clifftop setting, justifiably well-sung and much photographed and painted.

Further enhanced by the backdrop of Vesuvius beyond the Gulf of Naples, nowadays it is an immensely popular destination for cruise ship passengers. Its appealing centre, extensively restored since the days of the song, has a good offering of reasonably priced B&Bs and hotels such as Hotel Mignon ☎ 081 8073824 www.sorrentohotelmignon.com or Hostel Le Sirene ☎ 081 8072925 www.hostellesirene.com.

Tourist Information at ☎ 081 8074033 www.sorrentotourism.com.

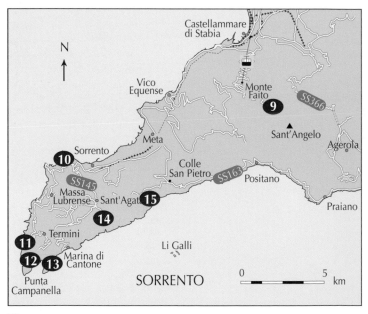

Back towards Naples is Castellammare di Stabia (20km from Sorrento), the departure station for the cable-car that ascends at a leisurely pace to Monte Faito, giving passengers time to enjoy to-die-for views over the gulf and well beyond.

From Sorrento itself, two key roads – both served by bus – traverse the mountainous peninsula that divides the gulf of Naples from that of Salerno. The Nastro Verde (green ribbon) swings southwest out of town to make its tortuous way around the point through farming land and hilltop villages via Massa Lubrense (Tourist Information ☎ 081 5339021 www. massalubrense.it).

Sleepy Termini is another feasible low-key base, with wonderful views across to Capri. It offers basic shops, cafés and Hotel Termini ☎ 081 8081041 www.hotel-termini.net. But more importantly the village is the gateway to the rugged promontory that terminates with Punta Campanella. Offshore is a protected marine reserve, www.puntacampanella.org.

What's more, a road via Nerano snakes down to a fortuitous dead end on the southern coast of the Sorrento peninsula. Here is secluded Marina di Cantone in a picturesque bay, a wonderful place to stay, well off the beaten track. It makes a brilliant base for local walks, though stray too far afield and the bus trips back get a bit too long-winded. Local fishermen unload their catches onto the pebbly beach and deliver directly to the string of superb waterfront restaurants, several of which are also hotels, such as family-run Hotel la Certosa ☎ 081 8081209 www.hotelcertosa.com, an ancient converted abbey. A splendid short stroll leaves the far eastern end of the beach on a path behind Ristorante Il Cantuccio. Swinging around the promontory over the sparkling sea it passes a ruined 16th-century watchtower en route to Recommone cove and a renowned restaurant with rooms, la Conca del Sogno ☎ 081 8081036 www.concadelsogno.it.

From Termini the road proceeds to the bustling town of Sant'Agata sui Due Golfi standing at the crossroads where the Nastro Verde joins the Nastro Azzurro (blue ribbon), the SS145, a more direct route from Sorrento. Located at 390m above sea level on the broad ridge separating the Gulf of Naples from that of Salerno, it has shops, an ATM and accommodation such as centrally placed Villa Titina ☎ 081 8780907 www.villatitina.com. Information at ☎ 081 5330135 www. santagatasuiduegolfi.it.

Looking out south to the Gulf of Salerno, the road continues east high over the rocky coast for 15km, transiting through Colli di Fontanelle, before joining up with yet another main route from Sorrento via Sant'Agnello at Colle San Pietro. From here on it becomes the Amalfi Coast – see the Positano and Amalfi sections.

Sorrento is a convenient base for visitors who can make use of buses, trains and ferries. See the 'Getting

There' section in the Introduction for ferry details. Buses venturing over the rocky peninsula to villages and the Amalfi Coast beyond come courtesy of SITA – timetables at www.sitabus.it. For information about Circumvesuviana trains from Naples via Pompei, some local services and the Monte Faito *funivia* (cable-car), contact ☎ 800 053939 www.vesuviana.it/web.

The rock pool at Bagni della Regina Giovanna (Walk 10)

WALK 9
On Monte Sant'Angelo

Walking time	3hr 45min
Difficulty	Grade 2–3
Ascent/Descent	530m/530m
Distance	11.3km/7 miles
Start/Finish	Upper station of the Monte Faito cable-car
Access	Alongside the Castellammare di Stabia railway station (on the Circumvesuviana line between Naples and Sorrento), is the departure station of the Faito *funivia*, cable-car; it operates on a daily basis all year. The upper station can also be reached by Circumvesuviana bus from Vico Equense, but while cheaper, is not half so exciting – or scenic.

Cloaked in beautiful beech wood, the isolated mountainous complex that takes in Monte Faito and Monte Sant'Angelo rises between the two gulfs, Naples and Salerno, affording 360° views taking in the Monti Lattari, the chain that makes up the rugged backbone of the Sorrento-Amalfi peninsula, culminating in lofty 1444m high Monte Sant'Angelo. Its complete appellation has the tag 'a Tre Pizzi' for 'three peaks', namely: San Michele, more commonly and confusingly referred to locally as the 'Molare' for its uncanny resemblance to a molar tooth; Monte di Mezzo, dubbed the 'Canino'; and lastly Monte Catiello, which was reduced in size when a huge slab detached itself in 2002, ending up in a deep valley below, providentially far from any human settlements.

The near-vertical, 1060m, eight-minute cable-car trip, with spectacular views over the bay to Naples and Vesuvius, is reason enough to come here. And after that there's the walk!

This walk visits the Molare, the highest point on the whole of the Lattari. It has a slightly exposed final stretch that rates Grade 3 but is easily avoidable – with a saving of 30min. Close by – and accessible for the average walker – is Croce della Conocchia, only marginally less panoramic, only metres lower (1376m) and vastly more comfortable to reach.

Good paths are followed but waymarking is a little scarce so walkers will need to follow directions carefully to avoid wrong turns; surprisingly few people make the trek up. While it is generally accessible all year round, unless there have been unusual snowfalls, late spring is lovely for the fresh greens, while a visit in autumn guarantees gorgeous orange-red-browns thanks to the beech trees.

Apart from the cafés and restaurants at the start, there's nothing else en route so take a packed lunch and plenty of drinking water. The walk makes for a long day when the travelling time is taken into account, so start out early.

The walk can be extended over the southern side with a descent to Santa Maria del Castello and Positano (see Walk 16). But be aware that this is a full day's walk and you'll need to have accommodation or transport organised at the other end.

The spectacular cable-car trip with views to Vesuvius and Naples

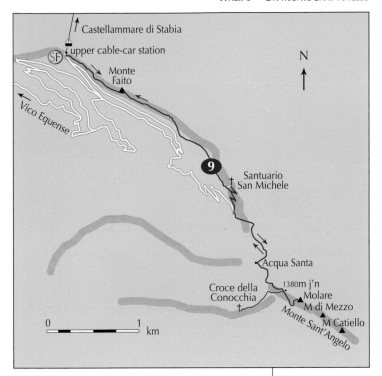

Castellammare di Stabia
upper cable-car station
SF
Monte Faito
Vico Equense
N
9
Santuario San Michele
Acqua Santa
1380m j'n
Croce della Conocchia
Molare
M di Mezzo
M Catiello
Monte Sant'Angelo
0   1 km

WALK

Once you've disembarked at the **upper cable-car station** (1102m) after the breathtaking trip, remember to check the time of the last return run so you don't have to spend the night here!

As you leave the building, turn L up the steps into pine wood to the sign for path n.36, 'Santuario San Michele'. This sends you SE along a crest with (more) brilliant views of the Gulf of Naples and the Sarno plain beyond. Red/white waymarks will be encountered at fairly regular intervals. ▶ A sequence of aerials is passed, but they hardly distract from the amazing outlook. The path proceeds parallel to a lower road which remains

The land below is thick with human settlement and even ancient Pompei can be picked out at the foot of the volcano.

81

The Molare is seen en route

out of sight, moving gently uphill through conifers and asphodels to **Monte Faito** (1131m). Further along at Porta di Faito (1205m), a lane dips into beautiful beech wood on a limestone base. Keep your eyes peeled for red/white markings and the path which cuts up L fairly steeply. It emerges on tarmac in the vicinity of a clutch of transmitters. Not far uphill L is **Santuario San Michele** (1278m, 45min), a church and statue. Rising from the densely wooded crest SSE is the distinctive jagged shape of the Molare (Monte San Michele).

Follow the surfaced road downhill – at the third bend turn off L through a grey gravel car park (the area is shown as Castellone on maps.) Cross the car park and turn L on a red/white path (sign for Molare) in descent SE through beech wood. Follow the waymarks carefully to a path split: keep on n.50 (n.00 forks L). A limestone ledge is soon reached and a corner rounded with an iron handrail. At the foot of soaring cliffs is the miraculous spring of **Acqua Santa** (30min) – the slits in the rock were the work of St Michael when he struck it with his sword; water still flows freely.

A little further on, the marked path veers sharp R to zigzag up to a key 1380m **junction** (15min). If the difficult route to the Molare doesn't appeal, then turn R for Croce della Conocchia (below).

Though there is no longer waymarking, fork L still in wood. After just a few metres the clear path crosses the main ridge to the giddy but breathtaking southern flanks of the Monti Lattari, where you begin to see the Gulf of Salerno. Not far along at a saddle turn sharp L taking extra care as the path is a little exposed, with loose stones underfoot. After a tiny Madonna statue amid rocks adorned by saxifrage and milk vetch, zigzag up to the top. Turn R at solar panels for the trig point on the **Molare** (1444m, 15min), crowning point of the Monti Lattari and indeed the entire peninsula. The reward is an amazing sweep of views all the way to Punta Campanella and Capri, then back to Vesuvius and the hinterland. Birds of prey may be spotted as they nest on the sheer cliffs.

Return with care to the 1380m junction (15min).

Now turn L (SW) as signed. Past a natural arch and aerial, stick to the marked path that keeps to the R side of the main crest. But as the iron cross comes into sight on the ridge above, leave the path to scramble easily up to **Croce della Conocchia** (1376m, 15min). ▶

Retrace your steps the same way back to the Faito upper cable-car station (1102m, 1hr 30min).

The grassy surrounds are dotted with delicate yellow orchids, but you'll undoubtedly be more interested in the sweeping panorama!

The view from the Molare to Vesuvius and Naples

WALK 10
Bagni della Regina Giovanna

Walking time	1hr 10min
Difficulty	Grade 1–2
Ascent/Descent	100m/100m
Distance	3km/1.8 miles
Start/Finish	Capo di Sorrento
Access	Capo di Sorrento is 3km west of Sorrento, a short bus ride with local line A (orange vehicle), or the SITA runs via Massa Lubrense.

Ever so short but so sweet – and easily reached from Sorrento – this walk is well worth it for spectacularly placed Roman ruins in a unique spot.

On a lovely headland looking out onto the sweep of the Gulf of Naples dominated by the looming bulk of Vesuvius stands a maritime villa constructed by the patrician Pollius Felix in the 1st century AD. The site encompasses a large natural pool the with remains of a landing stage, and the French Queen Joan of Anjou reportedly enjoyed bathing here in medieval times, giving rise to the site's present-day appellation 'Bagni della Regina Giovanna', 'Queen Joan's baths'. (On signposts the site is variously referred to as 'Ruderi Villa Romana', 'Roman villa ruins' and 'Villa Pollio Felice'.) Visitors can either clamber down for a dip or access the sea from the gently sloping rock slabs off the actual headland. The walk itself is straightforward and brief but plenty of extra time should be allowed for exploring.

WALK

From the bus stop at **Capo di Sorrento** (100m), opposite Bar del Capo, turn downhill NNW. Soon after a showy modern church you fork L off the road on a wide path with yellow waymarks and shaded by Mediterranean bushes, myrtle, broom and lentisc. With a gentle gradient it approaches old dark brick walls, the start of what's left of the sprawling villa complex (the locals bring their scooters this far.) The beauty of the spot is immediately obvious as the promontory opens up ahead, ancient remains smothered in flourishing green plants and aromatic everlasting blooms. Keep L around to a narrow rock neck and spacious platform with remains of the flooring of the villa (20min). The outlook is simply brilliant, over to Vesuvius and back to Sorrento, while below is the **Bagni della Regina Giovanna**, the beautiful natural rock pool in communication with the sea by way of a narrow passage.

Backtrack briefly and turn R under the platform through arched underground premises. You can clamber out onto the rock slabs, popular with the locals who fish and sunbathe there. When the sea's calm a swim is definitely in order. There's also a small sheltered cove L. Back

Vast view back to Sorrento

at the platform fork diagonally L on a narrow path with a wooden handrail that leads down to the natural **rock arch** over the pool. Cross it keeping R, and watch your step on the steep descent to water level (20min).

Afterwards climb back up – you rejoin the main path near the brick walls. Turn L to return to Capo di Sorrento (100m, 30min) and the bus on the main road.

WALK 11
Cala di Mitigliano

Walking time	1hr 45min
Difficulty	Grade 2
Ascent/Descent	320m/320m
Distance	4.6km/2.8 miles
Start/Finish	Termini
Access	Termini is linked by regular SITA bus to Sorrento, Sant'Agata and Marina di Cantone. The bus stop is in Piazza Croce where the walk starts.

In addition to the turquoise sea, the main attraction is a sea cave which you can swim into – or visit on foot.

It's well worth making this visit to the pretty cove and pebbly beach of Mitigliano on the western edge of Punta Campanella, a short distance below the village of Termini. Be aware that the descent path is particularly steep and tiring, though an alternative can be followed for the way back up if you don't mind walking on tarmac, thus making a loop. The cove has a sea cave which penetrates 70m into the cliffside and has a ceiling about 7m high. The water is especially cool and transparent thanks to an underwater spring, said to have shaped the cave. Lobsters are reportedly abundant, and are protected as this is a marine reserve.

WALK
From lovely Piazza Croce in **Termini** (320m) alongside the *Alimentari* (grocery shop) turn R down Via

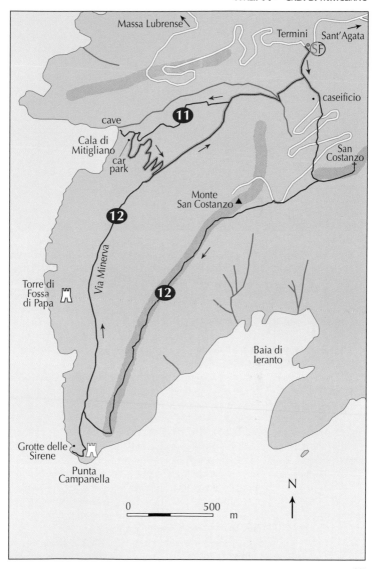

Massa Lubrense

Termini

Sant'Agata

SF

caseificio

cave

11

Cala di Mitigliano

car park

San Costanzo

Monte San Costanzo

12

Via Minerva

Torre di Fossa di Papa

12

Baia di Ieranto

Grotte delle Sirene

Punta Campanella

N

0   500
m

On the way down to Cala di Mitigliano

It's more exciting to swim in under the arch, but calm conditions are essential as waves can make it dangerous. The noticeably chilly patches in the water are caused by the underwater spring in the floor.

Campanella. A short way down fork R again to leave the residential area. After a stretch due W about 10min from Termini, as the road veers L, turn sharp R (WSW) onto narrow street Via Mitigliano, as per yellow markings. Close at hand is what's left of a 16th-century church, S Maria di Mitigliano, built on the ruins of a monastery whose monks were reportedly carried off by the Turks and condemned to slavery.

Houses and veg plots line the way which quickly becomes a lane, steep but thankfully shady. A path soon takes over, putting knees to the test. Skirting private property it descends between tall green netting and the edge of a dramatic canyon, glimpsed through gaps in the bushes. Watch your step. Below a gate and a small **car park** you finally stumble onto the pebbly beach of Cala di Mitigliano (45min) with a wonderful outlook to the isle of Capri. At the R end of the beach past a tower-like construction is access to the **cave**. ◀

After that lovely dip, if you can't face the near-vertical return path, take heart as an alternative is feasible: though surfaced, it sees little traffic.

From the beach, scramble uphill a short way to where a gate R opens onto a car park and minor surfaced road. It climbs in well-graded bends through olive groves and lemon orchards. Some half an hour up you join the route from Punta Campanella (Walk 12), turning L (NNE) in gentle ascent past Via Mitigliano and back to Termini (1hr, 320m).

WALK 12

Monte San Costanzo and Punta Campanella

Walking time	3hr
Difficulty	Grade 2–3
Ascent/Descent	510m/510m
Distance	7.5km/4.6 miles
Start/Finish	Termini
Access	See Walk 11

During their westward progress they tarried long about the headland of Athenaeum, which is the southern horn of the Bay of Naples now called Punta Campanella, and about its islands. A snowy temple, one of the wonders of the western world, rose in their honour near this wave-beaten promontory--for promontories were sacred in oldest days from their dangers to navigation; colonnades and statutes are swept away, but its memory lies embedded in the name of the village of Massa Lubrens.

Norman Douglas in *Siren Land* (1911)
(Delubrum means 'ancient sanctuary')

At the southwesternmost tip of the Sorrento peninsula and the culmination of the rugged chain of the Monti Lattari is wind-blown Punta Campanella, an important landmark for navigation. Once a temple to Athena, the Greek goddess of warfare and heroic endeavours, stood here, subsequently translated into Minerva for the Romans. Believe it or not – as nothing is left alone today – it was surrounded by fortifications and patrician villas as it also served as

This brilliant, rewarding and highly panoramic walk embodies masses of historical and legendary fascination and a beautiful range of wild flowers.

89

The 14th-century watchtower on Punta Campanella

an important trade post. The name *campanella* – a bell in Italian – reportedly comes from the gong sounded to warn of the approach of pirates.

Setting out from the laid-back village of Termini the route first climbs easily to a chapel on Monte San Costanzo. Again, in the words of Norman Douglas:

'The mists of Byzantium still cling to those grey rocks, for Saint Costanzo was patriarch of Constantinople, whose body, carefully packed in a barrel, floated from the Euxine into the Bay of Naples; it arrived fresh and uninjured.'

Thereafter the walk negotiates the wild spectacular headland. A lengthy descent ensues that's hard on the knees, but the path's clear. (Note: to avoid the long ridge route, set out from Termini on the straightforward lane as per Walk 11 for the initial outward stretch and come back the same way – allow 2hr.) After Punta Campanella a lovely lane leads back to Termini. Don't forget sun protection, plenty of drinking water and a picnic – there are shops at Termini. It's possible to fit in a cooling swim on the way back at Cala di Mitigliano, if you don't mind more descent and 1hr 20min extra – see below.

WALK

Lovely Piazza Croce with its ornate ochre-coloured church in **Termini** (320m) doubles as a belvedere with superb views to Capri. Alongside the *Alimentari* (grocery shop) turn R (S) down Via Campanella, as per yellow markings. At the nearby junction (where Walk 11 branches R) go L uphill on Via dei Monti. Pass a *caseificio* (dairy), some yellow waymarks and veer L and up old stone steps. Trodden by the locals for the July processions to San Costanzo, these lead out of the built-up area through vegetable gardens and orchards, cutting across the minor road several times. ▶ At a saddle curve L (ENE) up a broad grassy limestone crest dotted with serapias orchids. The modest church of **San Costanzo** (30min, 485m) looks out over the Gulf of Salerno and the Monti Lattari, as well as NE to Vesuvius. At your feet is the divine Baia di Ieranto.

Luxuriant flowering plants take over, a profusion of wild gladioli and asphodels together with stately pine trees.

Viewpoint over the Baia di Ieranto

Return WSW down the stepped crest, continuing past the path you arrived on at the edge of the *pineta* pine wood in common with n.00. A road is followed for a few metres; however, immediately after a fence around a vegetable plot fork L. Red/white n.00 marks soon reappear as you climb SW with spectacular views. An enclosure with military aerials is skirted, in the vicinity of the actual top of **Monte San Costanzo** (498m) and the fence corner touched on. Now begins the long descent on a clear path with a rock-earth base. While not kind to the knees it is extremely generous to the eyes as you follow the broad crest SSW with non-stop magnificent views dominated by the rocky island of Capri. ◄ The watchtower you're headed for finally comes into view, almost at the last minute. A track is reached – fork R across to a rough lane dubbed the 'Via Minerva', the ancient Roman route from Termini. Turn L for the last leg to the derelict but photogenic 14th-century watchtower and lighthouse on **Punta Campanella** (1hr 30min).

Spiky ferula, broom and asphodels alternate with rock outcrops and campanula blooms.

Steps lead down to a platform at the base of the building. Then, if you're not bothered by narrow dizzy places, don't miss the faint path R of the building to the narrow flight of steps all the way down to the waterside for three yawning vertical splits in the cliff where waves break and echo, reputedly the **Grotte delle Sirene**, abode of the renowned sirens no less! (adds 10min extra return).

Next take the lane N in gentle ascent, with remnant stretches of old Roman paving. Agave plants and lentisc line the way and a watchtower (**Torre di Fosse di Papa**) stands out below L, amid olive groves. Flanked by stone walls the lane improves and welcome shade comes from overhanging trees. After a showy limestone overhang, Termini comes into view as does a glimpse of the inviting cove of **Mitigliano**, far below. A winding surfaced lane that soon branches off is ignored (to detour to the beach, turn downhill L here and allow 1hr 20min extra – see Walk 11.)

It's steadily uphill past scattered houses on what becomes a little-trafficked road that continues E approaching the residential area. Near the village go L on Via Campanella and back to Piazza Croce in Termini (320m, 1hr).

WALK 13

Baia di Ieranto

Walking time	2hr 45min
Difficulty	Grade 2
Ascent/Descent	250m/250m
Distance	5.1km/3.2 miles
Start/Finish	Nerano
Access	Nerano is a small village in the SW sector of the Sorrento peninsula. It can be reached by bus on any of the daily SITA Termini–Marina di Cantone runs.

The Baia di Ieranto is a simply divine secluded inlet on the immediate southern flank of the mountainous ridge culminating in Punta Campanella. Smothered with masses of Mediterranean wild flowers, three rugged points jut out into the turquoise sea, offshoots of a single promontory. They host a photogenic watchtower,

The walk is a stunning straightforward circuit with plenty of interest and the chance of a restorative swim.

Magnificent view over the Baia di Ieranto to Punta Campanella and Capri

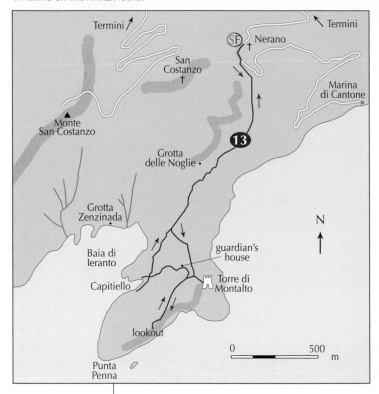

seagull colonies, a long-abandoned quarry and a handful of olive groves. The name Ieranto may be related to the Greek 'Jerax' for 'bird of prey': one hypothesis links this to the three-pronged outline, like a bird with outstretched wings. Nowadays, as the peregrine falcon nests on the Penna headland, walkers in spring are requested to stick to paths so as not to disturb the birds.

Take plenty of sun protection, drinks and a picnic if you plan on making this a full day outing. The tiny village of Nerano, where the walk starts, has a café and grocery store.

WALK

From the majolica-domed church at **Nerano** (169m) follow signs S to Via Ieranto, a matter of steps away. It is paved and in common with route n.00 for a short initial tract. Yellow paint splashes point S in gentle ascent through vegetable gardens, while wild garlic grows abundantly all around. ▶ The clear path leads across old terraces, amid lentisc, carob, tree spurge and olive trees. A pink gateway marks the entrance to the house where Norman Douglas is reputed to have written his inspirational *Siren Land* in 1905.

It's lovely going, scented plants all around and views over the sparkling sea L, while above are cliffs and caves galore, such as **Grotta delle Noglie** where evidence of Neolithic populations has been discovered. After rounding a point, the path drops a little; ahead is the marvellous vision of the Faraglioni stacks of Capri, and soon the Baia di Ieranto as well, not to mention the Montalto headland. After a house is a path junction where the return route joins up from the beach. Keep L and a short distance downhill is a FAI sign and map (Fondo Italiano per l'Ambiente – the National Trust who manage the old

Out to sea the distinctive Li Galli rock shapes stand out, and on the coast below is inviting Marina di Cantone.

The guardian's house and olive grove

industrial complex). Without going through the gate turn L (SSE) following a low stone wall and fence for the short climb to the 16th-century watchtower **Torre di Montalto** (Mortella) (110m, 45min). This wonderful lookout stands on the edge of precipitous cliffs – children should be kept close at hand!

Go back down to the wall, ignoring the path you arrived on, and keep L. In gentle ascent SSW you flank a well-kept olive grove and proceed high over the old quarry. The path narrows and the occasional yellow paint markings end near another wall. Continue in the same direction on an ever-fainter overgrown path SW. A little further on you veer L for a scratchy climb amid masses of purple orchids to an excellent **lookout** (134m, 20min) above **Punta Penna**. ◄

On view is Capri and the ridges of Punta Campanella, with the dark conifer patch of Pineta di San Costanzo and the eponymous chapel

Retrace your steps to the olive grove for a clear path marked by red dots forking L (N) through the trees touching on the guardian's house. Here traditional *pagliarelle* reed mats protect a citrus orchard. Take the steps downhill past an old lime kiln used back in Roman times. Soon turn L and down to a fork: L leads through to the interesting complex of old industrial buildings that once served the adjacent quarry (allow extra time for exploring). The quayside is also accessible, another good swimming spot though watch your step on the rocks. It's perfect for observing the noisy seagull colonies around Grotta Zenzinada on awesome cliffs in the neighbouring bay. ◄

Birds of prey patrol the area as well.

Back at the fork, continue L for the steep (watch your step) drop to the divine hidden cove of **Capitiello** (40min).

From the beach scramble uphill but take the rough path L (NNE) marked with yellow, an old flight of steps. It passes the derelict explosives store and amid huge domes of tree spurge climbs via a rock neck with vast views. The path junction near the house on the outward route is eventually gained: time for a breather! Now keep straight on, retracing the path followed earlier on. Admiring the lovely outlook onto Marina di Cantone and the southern coast over the Gulf of Salerno, you wander back to Nerano (169m, 40min).

WALK 14

Marina di Crapolla

Walking time	2hr 30min
Difficulty	Grade 2
Ascent/Descent	390m/390m
Distance	4.5km/2.8 miles
Start/Finish	Sant'Agata sui Due Golfi
Access	Sant'Agata stands on the SS145 between Sorrento and Positano, at the crossroads for Termini and Massa Lubrense. Many SITA buses from Sorrento and Positano come this way; they let you off in Corso S Agata.

One of the quaintest spots in Siren land is the inlet of Crapolla on the south coast. A rugged path, frequented by fishermen who bring their produce over the ridge to Sorrento and by a few bathing enthusiasts of Sant'Agata, leads down the incline, becoming more precipitous as it breaks away, perforce, from the stream which flows alongside, and which ends in a cascade at the back of the inlet.
Norman Douglas in *Siren Land* (1911)

Nothing has changed since the early 1900s when Norman Douglas wrote *Siren Land*, with the sole exception of the flight of steps, rebuilt a few years back.

A port in ancient Greek-Roman times, Crapolla is now an oasis of green where cell-like fishermen's huts cling to the rock face and a pebbly beach offers lovely swimming. The name Crapolla has been linked with 'Apollo', for an ancient sanctuary is believed to have occupied the spot. Nowadays you see the tiny chapel of San Pietro (St Peter), the apostle rumoured to have

Yet another must-do and yet another knee-jolting walk – 650 steps this time! Your destination is Marina di Crapolla, a tiny hidden cove at the foot of a dramatic 'V' of soaring cliffs.

dropped in here on his arrival from Palestine. It sports beautiful marble columns recycled from Roman villas in the aream, as well as traces of frescoes.

The lively township of Sant'Agata sui Due Golfi where the walk starts has shops and accommodation. The walk passes the outskirts of the village of Torca before a pretty path leads around the cliffs with gorgeous views over the Gulf of Salerno and a scattering of tiny rock islands, followed by the long staircase. Avoid climbing back up the steps in the heat of a summer's day as there's no shade! Later on the return leg a steepish lane route is given as an alternative to take you back to Sant'Agata.

Take plenty of drinking water and sunscreen.

WALK

From **Sant'Agata** (390m) walk S along Corso S Agata past a small park and the intersection with Via Reola. The shop-lined way leads to **Hotel Montana** where you branch R on a narrow street alongside the building (look for blue waymarks), soon forking L onto stepped way I Traversa Pigna. At the bottom of the flight of steps go L (SE) joining quiet surfaced lane **Via Nula**. A little way

Away from it all at Marina di Crapolla

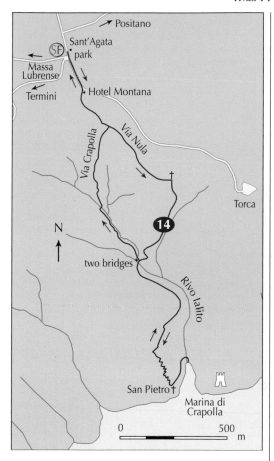

along ignore the turn-off for Via Crapolla, which is the return route. A slight rise and there are lovely gardens, olive groves and a brace of large Maritime Pines as you approach the village of Torca. As the lane is squeezed between a retaining wall and old houses take the marked fork R (S) at a **shrine** (blue and red/white waymarks). After a covered passageway the path drops quickly

The never-ending steps to Marina di Crapolla

through terraced gardens and light wood. It is faint and overgrown in places and all but disappears though thankfully not for long. You emerge on a clear stepped way (turn R), shaded by oaks and bright with red valerian and wild garlic. Further down this joins a lane in the vicinity of **two bridges**, modest affairs, over streams. You go L twice in quick succession to follow the bank of Rivo Ialito, on a level path high over Crapolla which is out of sight. ▶ Far R (SW) the headland of Montalto stands out. This is a stunning stretch high over the sea on sunscorched mountainside colonised by ferulas, giant fennel stalks. The red/white n.00 path breaks off R (W, for experts only) while your blue-marked breathtaking descent S starts in earnest, and legs get put seriously to the test on the steps. It's a relief to reach the chapel of **San Pietro**, an erstwhile Benedictine monastery.

Soon you are rewarded with wonderful sea views taking in the nearby islands of Isca and Li Galli.

The path now veers L into the narrow scenographic inlet **Marina di Crapolla** (1hr) shaded by fig and carob trees. Soaring 200m cliffs press in overhead, riddled with cavities. A tiny pebbly cove with upturned boats is backed by fishing huts, many derelict. ▶

An old watchtower stands out on the headland above.

After a swim and relax, retrace your steps uphill – preferably not in the middle of the day in summer – to the two bridges. Now ignore the marked route R (the way you came) and keep straight up (NW) on a concrete-based lane which soon becomes awfully steep. Passing through rural properties as Via Crapolla it reaches Via Nula where you turn L. Now, as per the outward route, it's along and back up the steps to Sant'Agata (1hr 30min, 390m).

WALK 15
Sant'Elia

Walking time	1hr 40min (1hr 20min if you have a car)
Difficulty	Grade 1–2
Ascent/Descent	220m/220m
Distance	4km/2.5 miles
Start/Finish	Colli di Fontanelle
Access	The village of Colli di Fontanelle is located on the Nastro Verde road between Colle San Pietro and Sant'Agata. Many SITA buses on the Positano–Sorrento run detour this way, otherwise there's a Circumvesuviano bus service between Sorrento and Sant'Agata. With your own car, drive as far as the belvedere (see below).

A gratifying short itinerary that gives a taste of the incomparable breathtaking coastline along this otherwise inaccessible stretch overlooking the Gulf of Salerno west of Positano.

Awesome rugged cliffs plunging hundreds of metres to the sea offer a plethora of nesting sites for birds of prey. A short way into the walk, not far downhill, is a rock tower once the natural pylon of a spectacular rock bridge that was immortalised in Grand Tour prints from the 1800s.

In the words of Norman Douglas:

'the once famous limestone arch, Arco di Sant'Elia, a portentous freak of nature. It is a sad wreck now, this once majestic portal opening upon the blue wonderland of sky and sea; the wind, which fashions the arches and pinnacles and melon-shaped grottos and all the bizarre accoutrements of these coasts, gnawed at the keystone till the span yielded'.

Nowadays even without the arch it's a great spot and the wealth of Mediterranean vegetation is always a pleasure. Surprisingly few visitors venture along the straightforward path. The walk start, Colli di Fontanelle, is

What's left of the Porta di Sant'Elia

a small village with a well-stocked grocery store, friendly café and restaurant.

WALK

At **Colli di Fontanelle** (340m), opposite Ristorante Stelluccia turn S off the main road onto Via Belvedere. This street wanders down to the belvedere (315m, 10min), which enjoys views of the tiny Li Galli rock islets in the Gulf of Salerno, as well as a good stretch of divinely rugged coast E to Praiano. Yellow paint stripes indicate a flight of steps accompanied by a wooden handrail bearing L (E) through vegetable gardens. ▶ Not far on, at a bend R a (broken) ceramic tile marker points out that this was the famous viewpoint for the amazing albeit long-collapsed natural arch.

Swinging SW in steady descent the beautiful path lined with rosemary bushes and carob trees leads past dizzy limestone cliffs. Punta Sant'Elia can be glimpsed SW. The next landmark is the romantic arched stone gateway **Porta di Sant'Elia**, once the entrance to a large agricultural property. ▶ The path continues through terraced olive

Shady oak wood bright with wild gladioli accompanies walkers downhill.

The portal was originally intended to defend against foreign invaders.

103

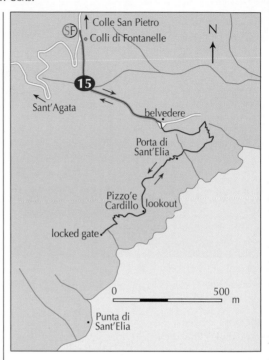

groves, marvels of man's resourcefulness. Overhead the near-vertical pink-orangey rock faces are pitted with cavities scooped out by wind and rain. The path climbs briefly across a drier mountainside thick with rock roses and tree spurge to a good **lookout** point beneath the **Pizzo'e Cardillo** rock formation. By all means end your walk here. Otherwise follow the path a little further as it plunges in zigzags, to an inevitable conclusion at a locked gate (130m, 45min), thereafter private property.

Retrace your steps. The return route gives you the chance to enjoy views of distant Praiano perched on the coast, while high above are the Monte Sant'Angelo peaks. It's then via the belvedere back to Colli di Fontanelle (340m, 55min).

POSITANO

The path climbs out of Vallone di Nocelle (Walk 18)

INTRODUCTION

On the southern edge of the Monti Lattari, facing the Gulf of Salerno, a dazzling cascade of pastel houses brightens a sheltered valley. Spectacular Positano got its name when Saracen pirates bearing a stolen 13th-century Byzantine icon of a black madonna were caught at sea in an awesome storm. A heavenly voice commanded them to '*posa*' or put the treasure ashore. Miraculously a gentle wind nudged the galley landwards, where the crew and captain were more than willing to hand her over to the local people. Naturally they built a church in her honour. She still dwells in Santa Maria Assunta, whose landmark majolica dome is visible from all over town.

Modern-day Positano is crammed with chic boutiques and off-the-scale starred hotels for the world's trend seekers. It is also perforce largely pedestrian, thanks to its near-vertical alleys and narrow stepped lanes.

Well served by SITA buses (www. sitabus.it) from both Sorrento and Salerno via Amalfi, the town has two key bus stops: in the upper western part of town 'Chiesa Nuova' is the first of these, encountered as you come from the Sorrento direction, while 'Sponda' is lower down on the eastern edge towards Amalfi. The lower district is traffic-limited and served by a tiny orange bus, 'Interno Positano', on a one-way loop Piazza dei Mulini–Sponda–Chiesa Nuova–Piazza dei

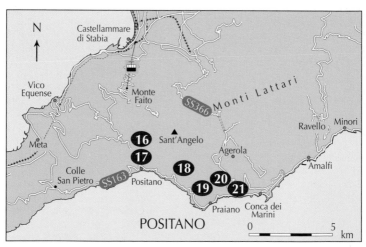

Mulini. Anywhere else is reached on foot. The local bus runs are managed by Flavio Gioia ☎ 089 813077 www.flaviogioia.com, and extend to the neighbouring villages of Montepertuso, Nocelle and Praiano.

A more relaxing way to reach Positano is by the ferries that ply the coast between Salerno and Sorrento – see 'Getting There' in the main introduction. Boats dock at a wharf alongside the lovely sandy beach.

In addition to grocery shops, cafés and restaurants galore, accommodation is available: options include reasonably priced, friendly and centrally located Villa Maria Antonietta ☎ 089 875071 www.villamariaantonietta. com, otherwise above the adjacent cove of Fornillo is Casa Guadagno ☎ 089 875042 www.pensione casaguadagno.it. (Tourist Information can be contacted at ☎ 089 875067 www.aziendaturismopositano.it.)

Villages with great views dotted over the steep hillsides above include Santa Maria del Castello (sleep at Il Rifugio B&B ☎ 081 8024114 www. ilrifugio.eu), and Montepertuso with its landmark 'hole in the rock' (B&B Le Ghiande mobile ☎ 339 7354765 www.leghiande.com). A local bus runs there, continuing on to Nocelle with Casa Cuccaro B&B ☎ 089 875458 www.casacuccaro.it and B&B Villa Sofia ☎ 089 811695 www. villasofia.org. This means really getting away from it all.

Another short trip by local bus along the coast road is to quiet Praiano (Tourist Information ☎ 089 874557 www.praiano.org) where accommodation possibilities include stunningly located Villa Bellavista ☎ 089 874054 www.villabellavista. it and moderately priced rooms c/o Trattoria San Gennaro ☎ 089 874293 www.ilsangennaro.it.

Just around the spectacular corner is a tiny cove and pebbly beach squeezed between cliffs. Marina di Praia is a cluster of whitewashed houses, cafés and restaurants dominated by the inevitable Saracen watchtower. It is also accessible by a flight of steps from Praiano. Buses stop on the main road for the short stroll down. You can stay at seafront Albergo Alfonso a Mare ☎ 089 874091 www. alfonsoamare.it.

Next comes tranquil Fjord di Furore, apparently in a timelock, unchanged for centuries. Visible from a road bridge and reachable solely on foot, this photogenic inlet appears briefly in the second episode of Roberto Rossellini's 1948 film 'Amore' starring Anna Magnani.

Conca dei Marini, 7km further east, is where the dizzy road across the peninsula from Castellammare di Stabia reaches the coast. En route it passes through farmland and mountain villages including Bomerano which is part of Agerola; Hotel Due Torri ☎ 081 8791257 www.hotelle-duetorri.it. Further down at Furore is La Casa del Melograno ☎ 089 8131311 www.lacasadelmelograno. it. SITA buses serve the route.

WALK 16

Santa Maria Castello to Montepertuso

Walking time	4hr 10min
Difficulty	Grade 1–2
Ascent/Descent	640m/720m
Distance	8.5km/5.3 miles
Start/Finish	Chiesa Nuova bus stop, upper Positano/Piazza dei Mulini, lower Positano
Access	The upper northwestern part of Positano is traversed by the main coastal road SS163, which goes by the name of Via Marconi here. The spot can be reached by bus: either the local 'Interno Positano' run or the long-distance SITA – ask for the Chiesa Nuova stop. Piazza dei Mulini is also served by the local 'Interno Positano' run.

A beautiful walk at the foot of the soaring limestone reaches of Monte Sant'Angelo on fine ancient pathways, arguably the best preserved mule tracks on the whole of the Amalfi Coast.

Mule tracks lead away from the hustle and bustle of trendy Positano, soon left far below, and regale breathtaking panoramas, even to Capri. In late springtime the route could be dubbed 'the orchid way' as chances of spotting the curious *ophrys* insect-mimicking varieties are good. From Montepertuso, in the latter part of the itinerary, is an excursion to Monte Gambera. The village name means 'pierced mount', referring to the yawning rock aperture overhead in Monte Gambera. Not a natural phenomenon, it was purportedly the work of the Madonna herself, part of her efforts to liberate the village from the influence of Satan. He'd spent a futile week attempting to perforate the rock, whereas it only took our heroine a flick of the wrist as she barely touched it with her finger (though in another version she kicked it out), a demonstration of her power over evil. Fabulous festivities

celebrate the event each year on 2 July, with spectacular fireworks on the mountain itself, to accompany the passage of the madonna – in statue form – as she rides an overhead cableway from the hole all the way down to the village church. It's well worth making the trek up there at any time – see below.

At Montepertuso it is also feasible to take the local bus to Positano, thus avoiding the walk's concluding descent and cutting 40min off the time. There are restaurants at both Santa Maria del Castello and Montepertuso, should a 'civilised' lunch appeal.

Near the Chiesa Nuova bus stop where the walk starts

WALK

The **Chiesa Nuova** bus stop (160m) in upper Positano is a tiny street corner crammed with shops, bars, people and traffic: all emblematic of the Amalfi Coast! Facing uphill, between the *Alimentari* (grocery shop) and Bar Internazionale, take the stepped Via Chiesa Nuova. This corresponds with CAI route n.33, which becomes n.3 further up and has occasional paint waymarks. You soon pass the church (Chiesa Nuova) and cross a road. Straight ahead is a ceramic plaque for walkers indicating the steps

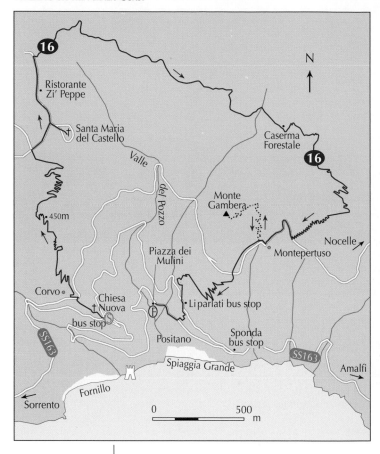

Views over Positano are excellent right from the word go, but they do improve with height.

of Via Corvo climbing N out of the built-up area. ◄ A rockfall barrier is passed and a cliff face followed; high above are 'inaccessible' recesses where small birds of prey like the Lanner Falcon nest. The perfectly graded steps are in good condition, making the ascent virtually effortless, leaving you free to appreciate the rounded form of Croce della Conocchia standing out NE on Monte

Sant'Angelo, and the gaping hole belonging to Monte Gambera lower down. ▶

Tight zigzags climb amid perfumed broom shrubs, and forks are ignored (including the 450m junction used by Walk 17). Shortly after a house and pylon is a quiet surfaced road with a sign for Il Rifugio B&B. Fork R through the rural settlement and R again at a wider road for the brief detour to nearby church of **Santa Maria del Castello** (670m, 1hr 30min). The views from its terrace space over the lush green wooded altopiano dotted with farms, and inevitably down to the sea, including glimpses in the opposite direction to Naples and even Ischia across the gulf W.

Retrace your steps to the last junction but continue straight on (N) past a bus stop and renowned **Ristorante Zi' Peppe** and its café. A little further on a series of lanes branch off R: you need the first one, signed for n.3. Soon, after a clutch of houses at the head of Valle del Pozzo, a path takes over in common with the Alta Via dei Monti Lattari (n.00). Soon swinging SE, this divine path is level for the most part and lined with cypress trees and orchids which appreciate the shade. At a fork (with a route from

The way is flanked with Mediterranean plants, mainly carob trees, holm oak and myrtle.

Broom frames a bird's-eye view to Positano

Monte Sant'Angelo), take the R branch leading through pine wood to a neat stone hut, **Caserma Forestale** (767m, 50min), a perfect picnic spot.

A clear stepped path begins, dropping ESE through flowered maquis vegetation. After a cleft chimney with a waterfall is a madonna shrine cave, an excellent lookout onto the gaping hole in Monte Gambera. Steps zigzag downhill, passing B&B Le Ghiande to the road where your turn R for the village of **Montepertuso** (365m, 45min) and its piazza, immediately after the Donna Rosa Ristorante. The grocery shop here sells tickets for the bus to Positano should you decide to call it a day. However it's worth making the short detour to Monte Gambera to visit the madonna's 'hole' from close quarters.

Excursion to Monte Gambera (40min return)

Cross the village piazza past Ristorante Il Ritrovo then turn sharp R up steep steps past houses and vegetable gardens. A level stretch L touches on the madonna's cableway then a final flight of steps lead up to the fantastic hole (500m) for dizzy views down Val Pozzo to the sea. The ladder up the rock face is for the volunteer fire spotters during the July 2 festivities when the vegetation inevitably burns! Return the same way to the piazza at Montepertuso.

From the piazza walk past the inviting terrace of Ristorante Il Ritrovo and continue SW on the level concrete pedestrian-only way. Immediately after a tobacconist ('T' sign) take the next L in descent across the road for the start of a broad stepped way between houses and lovely gardens, enjoying lovely views to Positano. It veers briefly NW beneath an immense sculpted rock face to a shrine marking the beginning of a steep staircase. This ends at a T-junction – go L for the gentle slope to join a cobbled street and shortly the main road Via Marconi (SS163) at the **Liparlati bus stop**. Across the road next to a grocery shop is stepped way Via S Sebastiano (sign for '*spiaggia*/beach') that cuts down to Via C Colombo where you turn R to nearby **Piazza dei Mulini** in lower Positano (80m, 50min), the terminal for local buses, and the walk's end.

WALK 17

Montepertuso–Fornillo Circuit

Walking time	3hr
Difficulty	Grade 2
Ascent/Descent	550m/550m
Distance	7km/4.3 miles
Start/Finish	Piazza dei Mulini, Positano
Access	The walk start in the lower part of Positano doubles as the terminal for local buses, in a traffic-restricted zone.

This wonderfully scenic circuit wanders high above spectacular Positano. Starting out with the inevitable upward slog on endless flights of steps, it visits the village of Montepertuso.

Meaning 'pierced mount', Montepertuso is overshadowed by a mountain with a curious yawning hole, source of a wonderful legend starring the Madonna (see Walk 16). A relaxing path leads through luxuriant wood at the foot of soaring dramatic limestone cliffs, a playground for climbers. This is a superb area for wild flowers, orchids in particular. A well-used mule track drops to Chiesa Nuova in the upper part of town and thereafter strings of steps descend through the cascade of pastel houses that make up Positano. After a well-earned pause at Fornillo beach,

The Spiaggia Grande and Positano

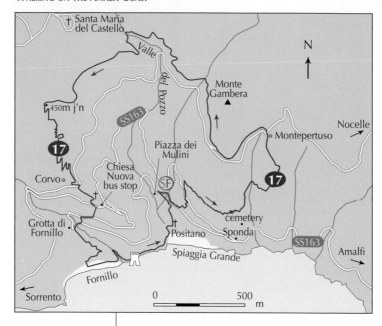

a short stroll concludes back in town. En route shops and restaurant lunch stops can be found at Montepertuso, Chiesa Nuova and Fornillo.

WALK

From **Piazza dei Mulini** (80m) turn up Via C Colombo. Some 200 metres along at a ceramic compass, branch L up steps (Via San Sebastiano) for the stiff climb to the main traffic artery Via Marconi (10min). On the opposite side of the road next to the Liparlati bus stop is a map showing the area's paths. Go up the adjacent steps and over a narrow road. Keep R to a short covered passageway and up to the road, turning R again. This immediately becomes a stepped way, passing pretty pastel villas. At a signed junction ignore the fork R for the *cimitero* and keep L, past the beautiful terraced gardens of historic Villa Croce, a handy landmark with its deep red facade. The way steepens as it approaches the cliff face above the town cemetery and traversing the olive groves of Grado it continues unremittingly upwards (NE). A swing R means a level stretch, which is, alas, short-lived. You finally find yourself in a low-key residential area on Via Pestella. Follow signs for Piazza Croce, below the church and through to the square of **Montepertuso** (350m, 45min), with cafés, restaurants, groceries and a bus to/from Positano.

Artistic ceramic path marker

Turn L through the square past Il Ritrovo restaurant and past the turn-off for the 'Buco di Montepertuso'. (See Walk 16 for the excursion to Monte Gambera.)

Keep straight ahead SW along the quiet alley to a car park and ceramic map sign. Take the R (higher) lane past sheet iron huts and up a couple of steps. A very pretty path, mostly level, leads through oak then pine wood alive with birdsong and views over Positano and ahead to impressive mountains. Ignore the branches R unless you're intent on rock climbing, and continue along wide ledges and over a stream. Gentle ascent brings you to a second stream in shady **Valle del Pozzo** amid luxuriant vegetation. Further along is the spring 'Sorgente Acqua Dragone' then a fork where you keep R below a vast rock face encrusted with limestone formations and multiple climbing routes. Soon a steeper path leads SW to round a superbly panoramic corner where the Conocchia ridge NE can be admired. ▶ Not far on is the 450m **junction** with the mule track from S Maria del Castello (45min).

The area is an explosion of wild flowers with red valerian, bugloss, cistis and orchids galore.

Turn L (S) in descent for the bends and zigzags of the enjoyable stepped way that affords gorgeous angles over Positano and the sea. Down amid the old houses of **Corvo** (160m) a minor road is crossed and you continue straight down steps. It's through the square housing a church where you fork R to the main road of Positano (30min). (Should you need it, the local bus to Piazza dei Mulini stops around the corner L at Chiesa Nuova).

Great views to the Conocchia ridge

Straight across the road is a staircase marked *'spiaggia*/beach'. It plunges between houses to a minor road – go R for a short way then L on steps again. Where you reach the tarmac in the vicinity of restaurants, go R to a wide curve and Grotta di Fornillo, a rock overhang studded with model houses and shrines. A sign points pedestrians L for 'Spiaggia di Fornillo', down SE through layer after lovely layer of guesthouses and whitewashed homes, draped with flowers. You emerge on the dark sand beach of **Fornillo** (30min) with bathing facilities, cafés and restaurants.

At the far L end of the bay take the steps for the pretty walkway past a watchtower to the ferry landing stage of Positano. Follow the path around the edge of **Spiaggia Grande** and turn inland at Ristorante Buca di Bacco. A series of stairs climbs to the rear of the church to a bougainvillea-covered alley lined with boutiques, to conclude at Piazza dei Mulini (80m, 20min).

WALK 18

Sentiero degli Dei

Walking time	3hr 10min
Difficulty	Grade 2
Ascent/Descent	310m/795m
Distance	9km/5.6 miles
Start/Finish	Piazza Capasso, Bomerano/Piazza dei Mulini, lower Positano
Access	Bomerano, part of Agerola, is on the important SS366 road linking Amalfi with Castellammare di Stabia and Naples. SITA buses provide a regular service both directions.

Legend says that the gods would descend here to the sea where the Sirens mesmerised Ulysses with their singing. It wends its dizzy way along man-made terraces hundreds of metres above the sparkling sea, linking the village of Bomerano with Positano. Limestone cliffs tower overhead, while below, the precipitous ground seems to disappear under your feet. Needless to say, magnificent views are enjoyed every single step of the way and you feel as though you're on the top of the world. Abundant waymarks guide walkers and the route is not especially tiring though the odd stretch on high can feel a little exposed. A word of warning: bad weather with strong winds could make the going dangerous so exercise caution and be prepared to turn back in adverse conditions.

Immensely popular and justifiably so, the famous Sentiero degli Dei or 'Pathway of the Gods' is everyone's favourite walking route on the Amalfi Coast.

The start point, Bomerano, is one of the thriving villages that go under the collective name of Agerola. They occupy a surprisingly flat expanse of agricultural upland on the southern margin of the Monti Lattari. Bomerano has plenty of grocery and fruit shops, as well as bakeries, accommodation and bus links. Further on, if desired, it is possible to bail out of the walk at Nocelle and ride the bus down to Positano, a saving on knees, not to mention

The Sentiero degli Dei affords dizzy views of Positano

1hr. Carry drinking water and a picnic, unless you plan on lunching at Nocelle, 2hr in.

An important decision awaits in terms of accessing the route. If you set out from Positano, where the walk ends, you'll need to change buses at Conca dei Marini; however the advantage comes at walk's end when you can walk straight to your hotel – or the beach. On the other hand starting from Amalfi means a single bus to Bomerano, then another direct if lengthy ride at the conclusion. Lastly, by overnighting at Agerola you'll be first on the trail in the morning and can make this a transfer itinerary to Positano if you don't mind carrying your luggage.

As another possibility, Praiano, which is easier to access thanks to its location on the main coastal road, makes an excellent entry point to the Sentiero degli Dei. However be aware that this demands an extra 500m in ascent. The outward stage of Walk 20 can be followed via Grotta San Barbara and the extension taken so as to join the main route on the outskirts of Bomerano, whereas Walk 19 slots in at Colle la Serra, looping back to Praiano later on.

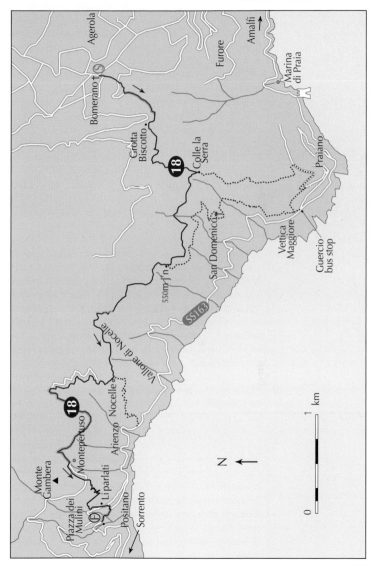

WALK

The main square, Piazza Capasso in **Bomerano** (638m), is recognisable from a distance because of the church. In a corner between two cafés is the sign for 'Sentiero degli Dei' (CAI n.27) which heads S along narrow Via Pennino. Not far on signs point you R across a footbridge and up to a quiet road where you turn L. ◄ Dizzy views over near-vertical vineyards accompany you to where the asphalt comes to an end, beneath bulging limestone flanks. A concrete ramp rounds a jagged outcrop which houses the **Grotta Biscotto**, its recesses used for farm storage. The route becomes a clear path proceeding W via terraces where vines and flowers spill over. ◄ Soon is an isolated rock pinnacle bearing a plaque in memory of Giustino Fortunato, an Italian statesman attributed with coining this itinerary's name.

The saddle **Colle la Serra** (579m, 40min) doubles as a junction with Walk 19 to/from Praiano. Branch R uphill on a narrower rocky path through a veritable maquis garden with massive bushes of rosemary, the delicate St Bruno's lily, tree heather and the omnipresent cheerful rock roses. The terrain becomes wilder and abandoned gardens with collapsed terraces are the norm; at the same time the route becomes more spectacular, and marginally exposed. ◄ Not far along around a point are exciting views to Positano nestling in its bay, its pastel-coloured houses cascading down the mountainside to the sea where bobbing boats are tiny flecks. A 550m **junction** and cairn (30min, where Walk 19 branches off) marks the start of a series of ins and outs, ups and downs leading NNW through cool wood dominated by holm oak and strawberry trees. There are glimpses of the crazy coast road below. At awe-inspiring **Vallone di Nocelle** the path climbs with a wooden handrail to the start of the pretty village of **Nocelle** (440m, 40min) and its narrow streets. Pass Casa Cuccaro B&B and turn R at the next intersection with a madonna grotto. (**Note** Ignore the signs in descent for 'Positano' unless you'd like to visit shady Piazza S Croce and the church, then embark on the 1700 knee-testing steps to the main road and bus stop at **Arienzo** – 40min.)

Aromatic herbs fill the air with their scent and broom and bright red valerian colours the wayside.

Overhead soaring cliffs are dotted with nests of birds of prey.

Ahead beyond the end of the Sorrento peninsula the legendary island of Capri can be seen while below is the spread of Praiano.

At Colle la Serra

After Ristorante Bar S Croce, if you don't opt for the bus to Positano (by following signs for *parcheggio* uphill), keep on the pretty path overlooking awesome cliffs. It curves round past B&B Villa Sofia to join the surfaced road (462m, 30min) for the stroll down to **Montepertuso** (365m, 20min). The settlement is overshadowed by **Monte Gambera** which features the rock hole that gave the village its 'pierced mount' appellation. Legend has it that the madonna pushed it out with her finger (or a kick) to show the devil she was the strongest – and rid the settlement of his evil influence! See Walk 16 for the short trip to the aperture itself.

Next to Donna Rosa Ristorante is the piazza where a grocery shop sells tickets for the bus to Positano should you decide to call it a day. Otherwise head past the inviting terrace of Ristorante Il Ritrovo and continue SW on the level pathway. Next to a tobacconist ('T' sign) turn L to cross the road for a broad stepped way downhill amid houses and pretty gardens. It veers briefly NW under an immense sculpted rock face, before a shrine and a steep staircase. This terminates at a T-junction – go L for to a cobbled street leading to the main road, Via Marconi, and the **Liparlati** bus stop (40min) used by the local run and SITA buses. Cross the road for stepped way Via S Sebastiano (sign for *spiaggia*/beach) next to a grocery shop. This cuts down to Via C Colombo where you turn R to nearby Piazza dei Mulini, lower Positano (80m, 50min), the terminal for local buses, and walk's end. Phew!

WALK 19
Above Praiano

Walking time	3hr 20min
Difficulty	Grade 2
Ascent/Descent	500m/500m
Distance	6.7km/4.2 miles
Start/Finish	Main bus stop at Guercio, Praiano (close to Hotel Villa Belvedere).
Access	Praiano is on the main coast road SS163 8km east of Positano, and is served by SITA bus lines which will deposit you at the main stop, Guercio. The district is also confusingly known as Vettica Maggiore. Otherwise by all means catch the local bus from Positano as this will drop you a tad higher up, at the church of San Luca. From there steps lead up to Via Costantinopoli, where you fork L on a paved way via a church and car park to the surfaced road to the main route.

Through orchards and woods this stunning rewarding circuit leads past spectacular cliffs with swoon-inducing views.

The ascent takes an old mule track still used by local farmers and their beasts of burdens to reach fields and terraced plots. High up, a beautiful section of the renowned Sentiero degli Dei (see Walk 18) is followed, while the return route visits well-placed Convento di San Domenico. Good paths are used throughout though be

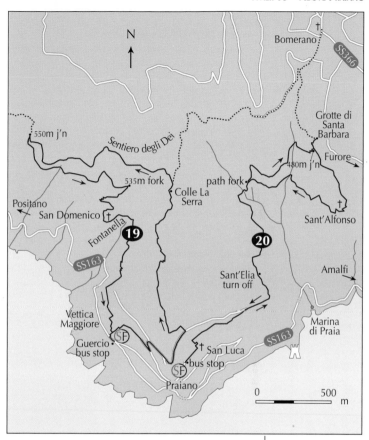

aware that there is the odd narrow stretch which feels exposed. The advantages of this circuit are that it is easily accessed and, apart from the middle bit, little frequented; moreover it returns to the start. But (wait for it) the 'bad news' is that it demands a stiff climb in between!

A longer loop is possible by following Walk 20 via Grotta S Barbara for the connection to the Sentiero degli Dei.

WALK

From the **Guercio bus stop** on the main road at Praiano (100m) walk NE (Positano direction) a matter of metres to the fountain in Piazzetta Gagliano, where pedestrian-only Via Russo turns uphill. Keep R at the ensuing fork to Via Roma. Go R along this alley, bearing L to join the upper road. Then it's R again onto panoramic Via Costantinopoli on a curve. Above an old church, not far along is a signpost at the foot of near-vertical steps heading NW (20min, CAI n.19). At the top of the flight, arrows point L at a junction as Via Colle Serra which levels out nicely, rounding a rocky point with a structure for the *acquedotto* (water supply).

Due N now the way is lined with carob, holm oak and olive trees not to mention scented broom, while views space along the lovely coast and over Praiano. Steps resume but with a much more decent gradient this time. Just before the 500m mark, terraced vineyards are traversed and a power line followed to (yet more) steep steps. Keep straight on at a fork with a tap, and past a house to a junction (a short cut L leads to a 535m fork

Mist on the path above Praiano

San Domenico is set high over Praiano

above San Domenico in 10min). Up through a pine copse is the strategic saddle **Colle La Serra** (579m, 1hr 10min) where the wonderful **Sentiero degli Dei** route is now joined.

Bearing NW/W the narrow rocky path ascends through a veritable maquis garden with massive bushes of rosemary, the delicate St Bruno's lily, tree heather and the omnipresent cheerful rock roses. The terrain becomes wilder and abandoned gardens with collapsed terraces the norm, and the way more spectacular if marginally exposed. ▶ Not far along a point is rounded for exciting views to colourful Positano and its bay. A prominent cairn marks a 550m **junction** (30min) where you branch L off the Sentiero degli Dei initially S. On a rock base it drops beneath an awesome cliff face to a perfectly positioned picnic table. ▶ The gently sloping path with a wooden handrail leads E to a fork at 535m (where the short cut slots in), at the top of the gully with the convent. Keep R through a rock garden bright with rock roses, zigzagging steeply SW/S amid spectacular limestone overhangs and

Ahead beyond the end of the Sorrento peninsula the legendary island of Capri can be seen while below is the spread of Praiano.

This dizzy stretch has vertiginous views over Praiano and its cultivated terraces.

125

caves. At a natural arch go R past orchards in a tight valley to inspiringly located **Convento di San Domenico** (383m, 40min), a superb lookout to the island of Capri. ◀

The church dates back to 1599 and is known as Santa Maria al Castro. It is the stage for evocative candlelight festivities late July– early August.

An improved wider path with old wooden stations of the cross skirts the **Fontanella** valley, descending easily S to enter **Vettica Maggiore** via an alley lined with tiny houses. At a junction with Via Costantinopoli turn R down Via Russo heading in the direction of a church spire backed by the sea. It's a short if knee-destroying distance down to Piazzetta Gagliano and the main road at Guercio, Praiano (100m, 40min) as the circuit is completed.

WALK 20
Grotte di Santa Barbara

Walking time	2hr 45min
Difficulty	Grade 2
Ascent/Descent	320m/320m
Distance	6.5km/4 miles
Start/Finish	San Luca bus stop, Praiano
Access	Praiano is on the main coast road SS163 8km east of Positano. Catch the local bus that starts out in Positano, staying on board when it forks off the main road at Guercio for the climb to San Luca in the upper part of town. Alternately use the SITA Positano–Amalfi bus, get off at Guercio and walk up the road – an extra 30min.

A beautiful loop walk that starts out in a pretty village and makes its way around a peaceful shady valley.

Here, amid woodland high above stone terraces built by generations of farmers and cultivators for their grapes and lemons, the interlinking rock cavities known as the Grotte di Santa Barbara make an attractive destination. Used as dwellings and shelter for centuries by shepherds and brigands alike, they retain plenty of atmosphere with

crumbling dry stone walls high up in the cave recesses. There is a tiny chapel, and talk of a secret passageway to the village of Bomerano hundreds of metres above. However access is for the surefooted only as it involves scrambling on an exposed cliffside, so is out of bounds to the average walker. This notwithstanding the site is still worth visiting. The walk starts and ends in Praiano and sees few other walkers, as the majority head for the famous Sentiero degli Dei higher up (see Walk 18). The outward stretch of this walk in fact doubles as an excellent alternate access for walkers if you don't mind an extra 400m climb. It is also possible to slot into Walk 21 en route.

Terraced mountainsides on the descent route

The paths followed are straightforward though the short stretch after Sant'Alfonso is a bit overgrown – this section is avoidable.

WALK

From the **San Luca bus stop** (180m) a paved alley leads through to the spacious piazza and church, whose truncated bell tower base is adorned with a colourful tiled scene of fishing boats looked over by a benevolent St Luke. Turn L up stepped Via Oratorio then R (NE) along pedestrian-only Via Pistiello coasting past well-kept gardens. There's a covered passageway and the alley changes name a couple of times. A stretch of minimal descent offers views to watchtowers and promontories along the coast. Olive groves line the way as you leave the residential zone on an old path bearing L (N). You enter a beautiful wooded side valley where insect orchids are not unusual, along with masses of pretty rock roses, scented broom, huge rosemary bushes and carob trees. Ignore the **turn-off** after 20min (unless you wish to access Walk 21, in which case turn R for Sant'Elia and Furore). Yellow paint stripes provide waymarking now. ◀ Tree heather and red valerian accompany you up to a small vineyard and **path fork** (300m, 45min), where the return route slots back in. Branch uphill on a broad stepped way bearing E across dry hillsides bright with rock roses and scented broom. After a narrow stretch through chestnut wood a stream bed is crossed and further up a 480m junction reached at a rock face. Turn L for steps that lead quickly up to an info board at the foot of the rock cavities of **Grotte di Santa Barbara** (520m, 30min).

The caves you're heading for are soon visible high above, NE, while voices from walkers on the Sentiero degli Dei will inevitably filter down here.

Extension to Sentiero degli Dei (30min).
From **Grotte di Santa Barbara** keep on uphill L (NNW) from the caves on the clear path to the minor road below Bomerano, where you turn L to join Walk 18.

Signposts point to Grotta dei Drapi a tight slit lined with stalactite formations. A route *'per esperti'* (experts only) explores the higher recesses. Be warned: it's a precarious scramble, as the original path has long crumbled.

Return to the 480m junction and go L (SSE) now. Keep R at the ensuing fork in descent through spectacular terraced orchards set amid soaring crags where birds of prey rest. There also happen to be marvellous views to the sea and Praiano. A road head is touched on near a rock climbing area. Fork sharp R here following signs for 'Agriturismo S. Alfonso', but keep L at the actual entrance

to the premises and past the tiny church of **Sant'Alfonso** (425m) in a lovely position. Soon a concrete ramp gives way to a lane zigzagging downhill. Take care at the second bend as you need to fork R for a faint path. (NB should you miss it, be aware that the lane, which soon passes beneath a pergola, ends at a gate and road, not shown on most maps. Clamber over the gate and go R (NW) to the farm to resume the main route). Next to a vegetable plot an overgrown path proceeds via terraces to steep old steps that drop to a dead end road and farm. Here a marked path resumes curving W back into Mediterranean bush to the path **fork** (300m, 45min) near the small vineyard encountered on the way out.

Return to San Luca (180m, 45min) and Praiano.

Sant'Alfonso in its quiet setting

WALK 21
Furore Fjord

Walking time	2hr 40min
Difficulty	Grade 2
Ascent/Descent	450m/450m
Distance	6.5km/4 miles
Start/Finish	Bus stop for Marina di Praia/Conca dei Marini
Access	Roughly midway between Positano and Amalfi, the cove of Marina di Praia is close to the main road SS163 and a SITA bus stop. An enchanting alternate access begins from the easternmost edge of Praiano where a flight of steps leaves the roadside above Torre Assiola. Hanging off the cliff edge, it drops to the beach where a minor road heads up to the bus stop. The beginning of Walk 20 can also be used as alternative access.

A beautiful picturesque cove in a squeezy tight valley only glimpsed from the main road, the Furore Fjord receives surprisingly few visitors.

The name Furore Fjord is said to derive – plausibly – from the 'fury' of the sea as it rushes in. For centuries Marina di Furore served as a natural port for the villages above and was home to a tiny fishing community. The old houses, recently spruced up, are called '*monazzeni*', from an ancient Greek term for 'living in solitude'. The freshwater stream which flows down from the Monti Lattari was later harnessed to power light industry and the old *cartiera*, paper mill, is a museum now.

The wild inner recesses of Vallone Furore are a nature reserve, home to peregrine falcons and bats, as well as the rare chain fern *Woodwardia radicans*. The valley reputedly also provided refuge for two famous figures:

The Furore Fjord

the bandit Ruggeri di Agerola who appears in Boccaccio's 'Decameron', and popular hero Fra' Diavolo, a leading figure in the struggle against the 18th-century French rule of Naples. The fjord itself gained fame in 1948 when neo-realist film director Roberto Rossellini shot scenes there for 'Il Miracolo', a dramatic episode of his film *Amore* starring the great Anna Magnani and Fellini in an unusual acting part.

The walk strings together three local itineraries that see few walkers, just sheep, herders and farmers. Waymarking is plentiful, mostly yellow paint stripes. The brilliant range of scenery encompasses both mountain and coast, secluded coves, wild valleys, woods and old terracing, where long stretches afford gorgeous sea views. As usual access is straightforward thanks to the excellent bus services. Praiano has accommodation, as do Furore and Conca dei Marini, while in the fjord itself is a laid-back café. The going is quite tiring due to the long flights of steps up and down. In warm weather a swimming costume comes in handy for a dip at the fjord and at the conclusion.

WALK

From the bus stop on the main road above **Marina di Praia** (75m), turn inland towards the arched bridge. Without crossing it turn R onto the 'Sentiero dell'Agave in Fiore' (path of the flowered agave). Aided by a wooden handrail, this begins a gentle climb NW in a shady limestone gully pretty with broom, valerian and lentisc and alive with birdsong. At houses a signed fork points you R and soon afterwards you keep R of a pylon. This sees you back in bushy surrounds, continuing N across abandoned terraces with minimal ups and downs. As the path curves around the valley head keep R at forks, proceeding between wire fences well beneath Colle la Serra and soaring rock faces. A stretch S goes to a dizzy rock point over Marina di Praia and its Saracen watchtower, a stunning spot. Around the corner (E) after a derelict house in an overgrown area, broad natural ledges lead through a veritable forest of prickly pear cactus and tall woody stalks of the wild fennel plant, not to mention olive trees that have grown wild. Concrete steps lead up through the patch of monstrous agave cactus that gave the path its name.

A pretty promenade soon takes over, bringing you to the piazza of **Sant'Elia** (250m, 1hr) and the exclusive hotel, Furore Inn. Only metres on is the start of an ancient way, which recently acquired the curious name 'Sentiero della Volpe Pescatrice' (path of the fisher fox).

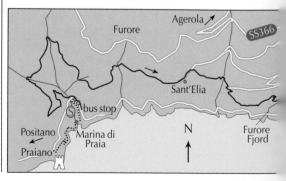

A staircase turns down R quite steeply past a water treatment plant. ▸ You descend into the cool recesses of **Vallone Furore**. Keep straight ahead on Via Roberto Rossellini for the magical cove of **Furore Fjord** (30min). The old fishing hamlet of Marina di Furore is a photogenic huddle of boats and old huts, a café-restaurant and a modest museum. It's a divine spot at the foot of soaring vertical limestone cliffs thickly coated with vegetation. At its widest point the valley bottom is 50m.

The path is a bit overgrown in parts, but generally clear. There's a heart-stopping stretch parallel to the sea, when all that separates walkers from a plunge is a (sturdy) concrete wall.

> **Exit from Marina di Furore**
> A flight of 200 steps climbs up to the road and bus stop for walkers who want 'out' at this point.

Cross the stream bed, which is usually dry, for the stepped way NE up the opposite flank of Vallone Furore. Keep L at the first fork then join a wider path (keeping L) with a handrail up to another mill building with water channels. This has been dubbed the 'Sentiero dei Pipistrelli impazziti' (path of the crazy bats). A turn-off for a near-vertical scramble to the Grotta delle Monache (nun's cave) is ignored. At a small waterfall the path veers R (S) leaving these cool realms. With views back to stalactite-studded cliffs, home to colonies of nesting bats it climbs to a **shrine** (215m, 30min) and lemon groves that announce the start

Café at the Furore Fjord

of a quiet road E. You soon leave it for steps R and an alley via the church of **San Michele**, before rejoining the road amid a blaze of bougainvillea and jasmine close to Locanda degli Agrumi. Next R, pedestrian-only Via Pali, leads to the yellow church of **Sant'Antonio**, continuing high over the **Grotta dello Smeraldo**. After a short stretch on Via Miramare, you need Via Lecina R. As it meets the tarmac, immediately R is Via Salita San Pancrazio, through olive groves. The eponymous church is a lovely lookout for Amalfi and Monte dell'Avvocata, not to mention a good place to rest those trembling knees. ◀ Via Croce is followed by a staircase which leads unremittingly downward towards the roofs of whitewashed homes. You finally emerge on the main road at Hotel Belvedere and bus stop at **Conca dei Marini** (75m, 40min).

Take heart, it's not much further!

For a dip, take either the nearby descending steps, or the following extension.

Extension to Capo di Conca (30min return)
Should you be in dire need of a swim in another divine spot, turn R past the hotel for the way down to the Capo di Conca promontory with its watchtower and café and ingenious bathing/sunning platform.

AMALFI

The steep staircase leading to Atrani

INTRODUCTION

Behind a seafront crowded with deckchairs and restaurants, and a ferry wharf heaving with tourists, is the historic heart of tiny medieval Amalfi. Crowded into the mouth of a deep ravine which extends a long way inland, it once had a system of defensive walls stretching across the mountainsides. In town, space is at a premium and motorised traffic strictly limited to a single street. Homes and shops are piled higgledy-piggledy on top of each other in a veritable maze of narrow alleyways and covered passageways that harks back to the town's Arab past. Shopping gets lugged up steep streets by hand, though mules are still the preferred form of transport for cumbersome objects – even fridges and washing machines! The square, Piazza Duomo, is dominated by a flight of steps, at the top of which is a striking landmark of a cathedral, with a chequered black and white facade and majolica domes dating back to the 13th century. Do find time for an exploratory wander around this amazing town to admire the ingenuity of the inhabitants, past and present. Amid tiny shops selling ceramics, groceries and the ubiquitous

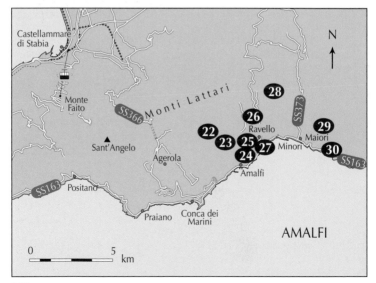

limoncello liqueur are elegant cafés where you can indulge in a pastry or *gelato*.

Inland, worlds away from the hectic coast, are quiet cool valleys offering lovely walks through an area that bears witness to the surprising magnitude of Amalfi's long-abandoned industrial past. However, these days a lower-impact activity is thriving on the surrounding slopes: visitors cannot fail to be impressed by the veritable forests of cultivated lemons. The uniqueness of the orchards lies in the way the citrus trees have been persuaded to act as vines, trained over pergolas and timber supports holding up the juicy harvest.

Amalfi's glorious past as a maritime republic is remembered each spring through a competition of rowing prowess with ancient rivals Venice, Pisa and Genoa, the 'Regata delle Antiche Repubbiche Marinare', which is held in rotation in the different ports. Moreover Amalfi is immensely proud to have been home to Flavio Gioia, alleged inventor of the magnetic compass, a godsend for early mariners. Historical research suggests that in fact he introduced this Chinese invention into Europe.

Amalfi is easily reached thanks to SITA buses (www.sitabus.it) from both Sorrento and Salerno. In summer huge numbers of ferries call in, with runs extending to Capri, but in winter these are limited. For details see 'Getting There' in the main introduction.

Suggestions for a stay include the smart seafront Hotel La Bussola ☎ 089 871533 www.labussola hotel.it or Hotel Amalfi ☎ 089 872440 www.hamalfi.it up a narrow alley. Otherwise inland at the start of Valle dei Mulini is charming Villa Lara ☎ 089 8736358 www.villalara. it. Tourist Information ☎ 089 871107 www.amalfitouristoffice.it.

At the neighbouring village of Atrani the church of Santa Maria Maddalena, in the upper part of the village, occupies an especially photogenic platform, immortalised by MC Escher in an inspiring lithograph. Hostel Scalinatella operates here ☎ 089 871492 www.hostelscalinatella. com.

Hundreds of metres above Atrani, on a lofty panoramic platform, stands the musical and cultural town of Ravello. It comprises relaxing, traffic-free, tree-lined avenues, elegant villas and wonderful gardens – outstanding are Villa Rufolo, and Villa Cimbrone with its famous statue-lined terrace. The spacious town square looks out to an ancient citadel, while its opposite extremity occupied by the cathedral. Inside this *duomo* is a treasure trove of relics: a fragment of wood from the cross, St Thomas's right arm, two teeth once belonging to the apostle St Matthew, St Barbara's head, and blood of Ravello's patron San Pantaleon, to mention but a grisly few.

Luxury accommodation abounds; relatively moderate options include converted convent Hotel Parsifal

☎ 089 857144 www.hotelparsifal. com. Tourist Office ☎ 089 857096 www.ravellotime.it.

The odd bus runs to Pontone where rooms can be rented c/o Blu Bar ☎ 089 872639.

Down on the seafront is Minori, which boasts the fascinating remains of a 1st-century Roman villa that has miraculously survived underneath modern-day apartment blocks. Just one of the coast's holiday villas built for the nobility of ancient Rome as a place to chill out, it has splendid mosaic flooring and frescoed walls whose colours are surprisingly bright.

Stay at centrally located B&B Palazzo Vingius ☎ 089 8541646 www.palazzovingius.it, Albergo Maison Raphael ☎ 089 853545 www. maisonraphael.com or Villa Marietta ☎ 089 852762 www.villamarietta.it.

Only kilometres away is Maiori, a resort since Roman times, when it was known as Reginna. It lays claim to the longest beach in this neck of the woods, backed by a plethora of modern seaside-type hotels. Tourist Info at ☎ 089 877452 www.aziendaturismo-maiori.it.

Amalfi's landmark duomo

WALK 22
Valle delle Ferriere

Walking time	4hr 15min
Difficulty	Grade 2
Ascent/Descent	620m/620m
Distance	10.5km/6.5 miles
Start/Finish	Piazza Duomo, Amalfi
Access	Amalfi lies on the main coast road SS163, and is well served by SITA buses from both Salerno and Sorrento. A short walk from the seafront is Amalfi's heart, Piazza Duomo, home to its landmark black and white cathedral.

The inland side of the famous seaside town of Amalfi is an amazing contrast to the crowded beach with its souvenir stands. A network of deep-cut valleys opens out, lined with row upon row of ingenious terraces which nurture the region's wonderful lemons. Hidden recesses cloaked with lush vegetation surround waterfalls and cascading streams, while high above soar impressive limestone cliffs. A full day should be allowed for this walk so that the varied landscapes and vegetation can be fully savoured. The valley's uppermost realms are in a nature reserve carefully managed by the Forestry Department to protect the marvellous flora and rare ferns, such as *Woodwardia radicans*, which flourish in a sub-tropical microclimate.

Valle delle Ferriere takes its name from the iron-working once practised there; the raw material was shipped in from the island of Elba. The fascinating old structures can be visited on Walk 23 which explores the valley floor.

Walkers should carry food and water as usual, however refreshments and meals can be enjoyed at Pontone near the start and Pogerola towards the end, where a bus can also be caught back to Amalfi if needed.

Looping around Valle delle Ferriere, this superb route also touches on pretty villages, and concludes conveniently back in town: a wonderful day's outing, one of the highlights of this guidebook.

WALK

From Amalfi's **Piazza Duomo** (6m), head N inland on Via Lorenzo d'Amalfi, crammed with souvenir shops, grocery stores and cafés. By all means walk up the R side, a covered passageway. At modest **Piazza Spirito Santo**, where it broadens to a 'dual carriageway' past the village **school** (the cream building with green windows), just before a tunnel, fork R up stepped Salita dei Patroni (CAI n.23). This climbs through a crazy jumble of houses and terraces, with washing hung out to dry, through a covered passageway to a level stretch. At a junction with a showy ceramic madonna shrine branch R up steps. It's steep going (just for a change!) as the way zigzags by way of fig trees and lemon terraces black with protective netting. ◄ Ascending steadily past modest houses, the route leads through an old masonry arch flanked by a shrine and multiple crosses. At a **junction** ignore the branch R (unless you plan on diverting to the Torre dello Ziro route – see Walk 24) and keep diagonally L. At the

An especially photogenic section hugs the limestone rock face.

The shady square at Pontone

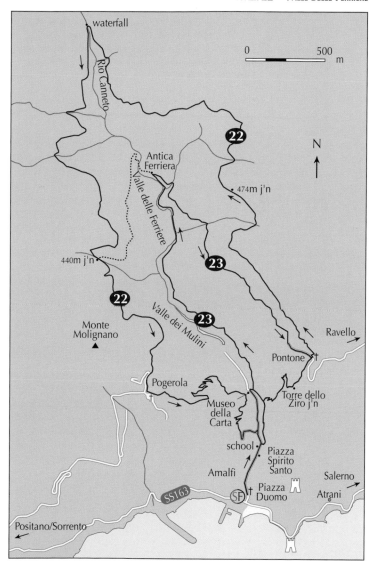

The quiet shady square doubled as an important wool market in the 12th century. Today children play on the precious flat terrain in front of the church.

nearby road, follow the sign for the *'centro storico'* of **Pontone** (266m, 45min). ◄

From the café turn up diagonally L past a restaurant then two taps. Yellow/black diamond-shaped waymarks grace the occasional power pole from here on, as do faint red dots to show the way. Up through a short tunnel the village is left behind as you proceed NW with lovely views over to Pogerola. Old steps lead through dense Mediterranean vegetation where carob trees and unruly bushes of heather stand out, though broom dominates on the perfume front. Sheep tracks criss-cross the area but the path is clear. ◄ After a hut for the *acquedotto* (water supply) is a side valley luxuriant with ferns and a swathe of pine trees, and dominated by breathtaking cliffs of pink-grey hues. The path enters a fenced area and at a three-way intersection you go sharp R to a **474m junction** and a sign announcing the nature reserve, then L. In common with a conduit belonging to the Acquedotto del Ceraso, the well-maintained forestry track coasts N then W along the 500m contour, approaching the cleft in **Valle**

Amalfi can be seen squeezed between lofty outcrops at the mouth of its valley.

Side streams are crossed

delle Ferriere. In dense cool wood the path reaches cascading **Rio Canneto** and a beautiful **waterfall** (450m, 1hr 20min). Take care to branch immediately L here (**without** continuing uphill to a second fall) and ford the stream. Yellow paint blobs show the way across wide ledges above kettle drums sculpted out of the bedrock by flowing water. Regular red/white markings (CAI n.59) take over as you pass a ruined lime kiln and curve through a side valley with a stream. Immediately afterwards fork R in ascent through masses of purple orchids to a lookout to the sea. Head-high grasses and ferns precede a drop across another minor stream. Soon dry stone walls line the way through chestnut wood to a path **junction** (440m, 40min)

Return to Amalfi via Valle dei Mulini (1hr 15min)
Here it is possible to turn off in descent, in common with the 'Sentiero Giustino Fortunato'. It drops steeply through wood to Valle dei Mulini and continues to Amalfi – see the first half of Walk 23 in reverse.

Keep on S following a fence below Monte Molignano to a vaulted stone hut labelled 'L'Oasi del Cacciatore' ('hunter's oasis') in a beautifully scenic position over cultivated fields. Soon afterwards the path veers L plunging down an old stepped way lined with tall stone walls then a wooden railing and into the village. Soon, past Trattoria Rispoli, is the tiny piazza of **Pogerola** (305m, 45min), which boasts a delicious cool drinking fountain, café/ *gelateria* and a bus link to Amalfi. ▶

Erstwhile Castrum Pigellulae, this was once a strategic part of the extensive defensive walls around Amalfi.

However you need to take the last alley on the L immediately **before** the square; this makes its lovely way E via a knee-testing stone staircase through shady wood overlooking **Valle dei Mulini** and its string of old paper mills. Swinging in wide curves, it finally reaches the road and **Piazza Santo Spirito**. Here you fork R to re-enter Amalfi and **Piazza Duomo** (6m, 45min) where relaxing cafés beckon, not to mention the beach.

WALK 23

Valle dei Mulini and Pontone

Walking time	2hr 10min
Difficulty	Grade 1–2
Ascent/Descent	260m/260m
Distance	6km/3.7 miles
Start/Finish	Piazza Duomo, Amalfi
Access	See Walk 22

The walk explores a romantic valley before continuing on a panoramic mule track to the sun-soaked village of Pontone, where a memorable path returns to Amalfi: a highly recommended 'must-do', suitable for all walkers.

Squashed in between craggy limestone cliffs, Amalfi shelters in the mouth of the valley of Rio Canneto. It peeks out of this effective hideaway at the sea, central to its seafaring past. However at the 'rear', hidden from sight worlds away from the hectic coast, is magical Valle dei Mulini. The name, 'valley of the mills', refers to the town's long-standing papermaking trade, practised there from the Middle Ages up to the 1950s, often using rags as raw material. In the upper part of the valley, which has a different name, Valle delle Ferriere, iron working was practised: nails and iron plates were the main products. The industry has been long abandoned, and it is now a beautiful nature area.

A link is given with Walk 22 and the Valle delle Ferriere circuit – see below.

WALK

At Amalfi's **Piazza Duomo** (6m) follow the main street, Via Lorenzo d'Amalfi, crammed with shops selling everything from *gelato* to groceries, as it heads N inland. Keep to the R side via the atmospheric whitewashed passageway. The road widens marginally at minuscule **Piazza Spirito Santo** and a **school** building, then passes under a short tunnel. As Via Marino del Giudice, it passes villas and the first of the old *cartiere* paperworks. ◄ At the interesting Museo della Carta, housed in medieval premises, turn R off the main road and leave the valley floor. A short way up veer L for steps before the gates of another school, and leave the

Underfoot you hear the gushing of the covered river.

At the Antica Ferriere

residential area. There are lovely views over to Pogerola as you proceed NNW on Via Paradiso climbing gently past a church and over an immense sea of lemons and vegetable plots. Soon a curious fascist-era water intake is linked to channels that supplied the old mills. Penetrating the **Valle dei Mulini** alongside cascading Rio Canneto, the way becomes stony and the setting wilder as cliffs close in. The first of a series of derelict buildings occupies an evocative setting and is all but invaded by wild fig trees and valerian sprouting from cracks in the masonry. Further along this beautiful path steps lead to the **Antica Ferriere** (240m, 1hr), a shady green romantic spot. Take time out to explore the extensive ruins. Should you wish to proceed to Pogerola on Walk 22, use the following link.

Link to Valle delle Ferriere walk
Keep on uphill following the stream NW and cross it L on a rudimentary footbridge. A clear path continues along an old channel to where a branch R ends at a locked gate (to the Riserva); however you fork L on 'Sentiero Giustino Fortunato'. A fainter path, it climbs steadily S through wood to the fence and **440m junction** in chestnut wood in Walk 22 (40min).

The staircase dropping to Amalfi

At a picnic table is the Pontone junction – fork R (SE) on an old way with a wooden handrail. In light wood it ascends gently below soaring cliffs, in due course reaching a saddle amid lemon orchards with a lovely view to Amalfi. A quiet surfaced road takes over into **Pontone** (260m, 40min).

Immediately after a car park, detour L (sign for *centro storico*) to the tiny market square and church as well as al fresco cafés and restaurants should you be in need of restoration. In addition, Walk 24 to the Torre di Ziro can be picked up there. Otherwise it's sharp R for the spectacular albeit knee-testing way, initially stepped, through cleverly terraced well-tended orchards. Ignore turn-offs and keep relentlessly downwards in steep zigzags, ducking under an awesome limestone overhang. At a T-junction at the start of the residential area, turn L, thankfully on a level for a while parallel to the valley floor. Through a covered archway with a madonna shrine it's finally down to the road where you fork L through **Piazza Spirito Santo**. It's only a short stroll back to Amalfi's **Piazza Duomo** (30min, 6m).

WALK 24

Torre dello Ziro

Walking time	1hr 30min
Difficulty	Grade 1–2
Ascent/Descent	150m/150m
Distance	3km/1.8 miles
Start/Finish	Pontone
Access	About halfway up the access road to Ravello is the turn-off for Pontone; occasional buses come up from Amalfi. However a more enjoyable way to reach it is on foot from Amalfi in 45min – see Walk 22. Below the actual village, branch off the path immediately after the arch with the crosses. This will quickly bring you to the main route a short distance from the church of Santa Maria del Carmine.

The destination of this short but highly recommended walk is an ancient watch tower in a commanding position on a narrow spur on the southernmost verge of Monte Aureo, high over Amalfi and Atrani. The Arab appellation 'ziro' refers to its cylindrical shape, like that of the containers once used for storing oil or cereals. It was built in 1480 on the ruins of a castle, still visible, and belonged to the vital system of defensive walling around Amalfi, which stretched up to Pogerola perched on cliffs opposite.

The tower became the tragic prison for the hapless duchess of Amalfi, Joan of Aragon. Unjustly dubbed 'La Pazza' (madwoman), she became a focus for scandal mongering, and was executed there together with her children in the early 1500s.

This walk to Torre dello Ziro is straightforward on clear paths. Lunch is available at Pontone's cafés and restaurants.

Torre dello Ziro and fortifications over the sea

WALK

From the tiny square at **Pontone** (260m), go under the arch alongside the church and turn R past restaurants to the motorable road. Straight over the other side a staircase (signed for Torre dello Ziro) leads down past the church of **Santa Maria del Carmine**. It is soon joined by the direct path from Amalfi and embarks on tight stepped curves up a rock face to enter the realms of the castle itself. Here a belvedere terrace looks out E to Villa Cimbrone and Ravello. An unsightly concrete structure precedes a clearing (where the return route slots back in) – turn L in descent through scented pine wood below the actual ridge. At an outcrop, ignore the fork uphill (used on the return route) and continue S with ever-improving views over Valle del Dragone to the dizzy promontory that is home to **Torre dello Ziro** (185m, 40min). ◄

Saturated with the mesmerising outlook, backtrack to the outcrop and fork diagonally L uphill in the company of cypress trees. At the top continue in the same direction to another wonderful **belvedere** with a concrete **pillar**. Then turn back, but continue along the top now (N) to where a stepped way L leads past old water cisterns and

An old walkway to a fortified corner gives even better bird's-eye angles onto both Atrani and Amalfi.

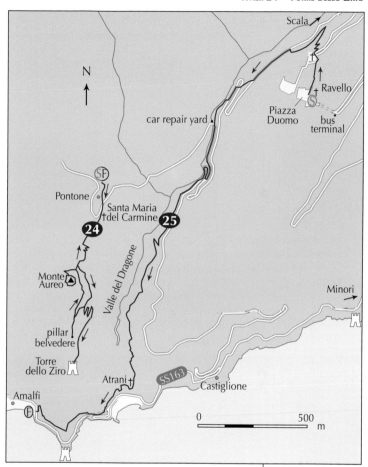

up to the very top of **Monte Aureo** to what's left of the castle walls and internal structures, crumbling and overgrown. The path circles the promontory before leading down to the clearing encountered on the way in. It's now a matter of exiting the old castle premises and returning to **Pontone** the way you came in (260m, 50min).

WALK 25
Ravello to Amalfi via Valle del Dragone

Walking time	1hr 15min
Difficulty	Grade 1–2
Descent	350m
Distance	3.5km/2.2 miles
Start/Finish	Piazza Duomo, Ravello/Piazza Duomo, Amalfi
Access	Ravello is served by a steady stream of buses from the coast road and Amalfi, 6.4km away. From the bus terminal walk through the tunnel to Piazza Duomo.

For route map, see Walk 25.

Setting out from Ravello, this easy walk explores the Valle del Dragone and can be linked with Walk 27 at either Atrani or Ravello.

Sophisticated and utterly charming Ravello occupies a lush elevated platform 350 metres above sea level. Backed by the rugged Monti Lattari, it is a peaceful traffic-free haven of narrow lanes and alleys, villas and gardens where hours can happily be spent wandering in exploration. Lovely cafés set on divinely scenic terraces overlooking the sparkling coast invite passers-by for a

Bird's-eye view of Atrani squeezed between cliffs

Terraced cliffs above Valle del Dragone

leisurely drink. Before setting out in any direction, pick up a free town map from the helpful Tourist Office close to the cathedral.

The old paved way along Valle del Dragone was the strategic access route for Ravello until 1930, when the surfaced road was built. It's an easy descent and, once down at sea level in the delightful village of Atrani, the route continues through a veritable maze of alleys, houses and churches to its conclusion on the seafront at Amalfi.

WALK

At Ravello, in **Piazza Duomo** (359m) face the cathedral and turn L (N) along a broad alley, Via Roma. Just before the Tourist Office (and a dead end) bear L towards the church of Santa Maria a Gradillo. Take the steps flanking the far side of the building and cross a road for the staircase, Via Sigilgaida, signed for Atrani. Go L at the next fork to join the main road. A short distance downhill a well-signed series of steps cut hairpin bends, becoming a lovely shady way alongside a stream below road level. An arched passageway under houses reaches a **car repair yard** (*carrozzeria*),

151

High above is Pontone and the wooded promontory where Torre dello Ziro stands out. Below the sheer cliffs, vines are cultivated in handkerchief-size plots of arable land.

then the quiet Pontone road. Where this joins the busier Ravello road, turn R past a ceramics sales outlet to the concrete ramp at the start of Via Valle del Dragone, the original way to the coast. ◄

The ruined buildings dotted along the valley made up the erstwhile industrial zone of Atrani, which harnessed power from the watercourse. Approaching the village the way steepens, entering a labyrinth of passages and narrow streets. You can't really go wrong as all roads inevitably end up at Piazza Umberto I in **Atrani** (45min). This lively square is lined with cafés and eateries, and there's access to the beach under the arch of the elevated road. ◄

Squeezed between buildings is the San Salvatore de Birecto where the doges of the ancient Republic of Amalfi used to be proclaimed.

To continue to Amalfi, cross the square to Osteria Luisella, and enter the dark narrow tunnel to its R. This emerges amid whitewashed houses where you need to keep an eye out for the rare 'Amalfi' arrows, as you climb a little, parallel to the main road (SW). A concrete wall edges the way, leading around a corner overlooking a Saracen watchtower. Then it's through an atmospheric string of tunnel alleys and steps, and you finally reach the road at the E end of the beach not far from the Tourist Office at **Amalfi** (4m, 30min).

Atrani seen from the path to Amalfi

WALK 26
Ravello and Santa Caterina Loop

Walking time	2hr 30min
Difficulty	Grade 1–2
Ascent/Descent	350m/350m
Distance	7km/4.3 miles
Start/Finish	Piazza Duomo, Ravello
Access	Frequent buses leave Amalfi for the 30min run up to hilltop Ravello. From the terminal, walk through the tunnel to Piazza Duomo and the town's cathedral.

According to legend, in AD339, a party of patrician Roman families were on their way to Constantinople, the new capital, and took shelter on the Amalfi Coast from a furious storm. So amenable and easily defendable was it that they stayed on. The very first village settled was Scala. Nowadays it is overshadowed by Ravello, but the cluster of six remaining hillside villages is quietly charming: Minuta, Campidoglio, Santa Caterina, San Pietro, Pontone and Scala itself. They are explored in this appealing circuit which starts out from marvellous Ravello, set on a lofty platform just a short way from Amalfi yet well away from coastal chaos.

Peaceful Pontone is a great spot for a village lunch if you haven't brought your own. Here too you can slot into several walks and vary the return by branching off to Valle delle Ferriere, Torre dello Ziro, Atrani or Amalfi – see below.

Note: as will be quickly become clear in the description below, most of this walk follows roads. However far from being trafficked thoroughfares these almost exclusively mean surfaced pedestrian-only lanes along with stepped ways that have served the hillside towns and villages for centuries.

Leaving behind the villas and exclusive hotels of the sophisticated town of Ravello, this delightful walk heads around to memorable panoramas by way of lanes and steep staircases.

WALK

From **Piazza Duomo**, Ravello (359m) take Via E. Filiberto, a leisurely broad stepped way past the former hotel where Escher stayed in 1923. At the top, where it is called Via Wagner, go L (N) past the **Municipio** and along to the superb Belvedere Principessa di Piemonte where a photographic detour is warranted. Luxury hotels and ornate villas accompany you through to the 11th-century church in Piazza San Giovanni del Toro for the lane forking R (Via S Margherita). A gentle downhill stretch overlooks wooded mountains taking in San Nicola and the Monte dell'Avvocata ridge.

A brief bit of surfaced road leads via the lovely moorish fountain in **Piazza Fontana Moresca** to Hotel Bonadies. Keep straight on (NNE) gently uphill through former fortifications and a gateway to Ravello, into Piazza Mansi and the church of **Lacco** (15min).

Flanking lovely gardens, proceed along Via Trifone through the residential area, but where it forks R, keep on the L (NW) branch Via Casa Bianca, a surfaced lane. This in turn becomes Via Grotta di Campo, curving over dark

Belvedere Principessa di Piemonte at Ravello

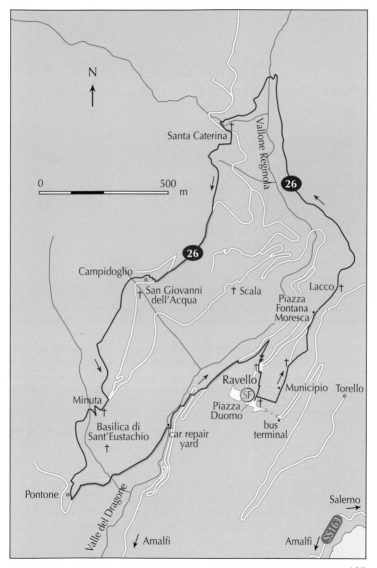

N

Santa Caterina

Vallone Reginola

0   500 m

26

Campidoglio

26

San Giovanni
dell'Acqua

† Scala

Lacco †

Piazza
Fontana
Moresca

Ravello

Municipio   Torello

SF

Minuta †

Piazza
Duomo

bus
terminal

Basilica di
Sant'Eustachio
†

car repair
yard

Pontone

Salerno

Valle del Dragone

↓ Amalfi

Amalfi ↓

SS163

The village of Campidoglio

green wooded **Vallone Reginola** and looking to the church of San Pietro. Houses are finally left behind as a dirt path coasts N through oak wood and a farm. Paving takes over past several circular ruins, lime kilns in all probability. Immediately after the second structure fork L on a path in gentle descent towards the valley floor thick with ferns and chestnut trees. You curve L onto a wider path across the stream then up the other side past farms to the landmark white church of **Santa Caterina** (448m, 1hr).

Opposite the building take the narrow asphalt road uphill and turn off second R up stairs past houses with the odd faint red paint marks. Bear L downhill, keeping R at a fork along a high stone wall. This soon curves L as a lane with lovely views to Monte dell'Avvocata then Ravello spread along its promontory punctuated with churches and parks. Passing farms, you cross a road and the lane continues in parallel, narrowing to a path high above the cathedral of Scala. Steps lead up to the asphalt and an intersection where you keep L into **Campidoglio**. As the pretty church of **San Giovanni dell'Acqua** comes into sight close at hand, branch R up stairs to a lovely level stretch past drinking water and a shrine to John the Baptist. Soon a concreted path bears SSW. ◄ Further on, at an intersection with a flight of stairs and a signboard, fork L to clunk your steep way through rural properties to **Minuta**. Keep R down to the pretty square complete with old church and fountain. Below is the landmark skeleton of 12th-century **Basilica di Sant'Eustachio**. Fork R down an old paved way and later L under an arch and ancient vaults preceding the piazza of **Pontone** (260m, 45min) for cafés and restaurants.

There are magnificent sweeping views to the Villa Cimbrone gardens and beyond.

Extensions
From here you can proceed to Valle delle Ferriere (Walk 22), Amalfi (Walk 23) or Torre del Ziro (Walk 24)

Turn L under the arch and immediately L past the public loo. Yellow waymarks soon point you R down to the road (unfortunately the old way marked on maps is no longer feasible). Go L through two short tunnels, then at the bend and **car repair yard** (*carrozzeria*) in Valle del Dragone, fork L under the houses to cool woodland.

Exit to Atrani
It is possible to turn R at the *carrozzeria* for Atrani – see Walk 25.

Steps climb to the road for a series of well-signed short cuts. Further up you need the fork for 'Ravello *centro*'. At the start of Ravello and Via Sigilgaida take the steps L of the church then R along the alley lined with ceramic shops and jasmine back to **Piazza Duomo** (359m, 45min).

WALK 27
Minori–Atrani–Amalfi

Walking time	1hr 50min
Difficulty	Grade 1–2
Ascent/Descent	250m/250m
Distance	4.2km/2.6 miles
Start/Finish	Minori seafront/Amalfi seafront
Access	Minori is a 3km SITA bus trip east of Amalfi on the SS163.

Don't miss this wonderful walk! This stunning route is a sequence of orchards, pretty villages and spectacular views – not to mention never-ending staircases.

Though just under 2hr is given, this unmissable walk will undoubtedly take much longer due to the lure of frequent photo stops and the inviting cafés and beach at Atrani. Moreover it can be extended to Ravello where Walk 25 can be picked up for a different route to Atrani (see below).

Close to the start at the seaside town of Minori are the fascinating ruins of a 1st-century Roman holiday villa deep below street level. See Walk 28 for more.

WALK

From the western end of the seafront promenade at **Minori** (5m), is Piazzale Marinai d'Italia with a madonna shrine. Facing the cliffs, don't be tempted by the staircase diagonally L (it's a dead end), but opt for the next stepped alley, Via S. Giovanna a Mare. It ascends steeply W past houses and the eponymous church, before crossing the road for a narrow staircase with yellow waymarks. Great panoramas can be enjoyed at every twist and turn of this near-vertical way that passes the town **cemetery**, an oasis of greenery and peace. For the time being follow the ceramic tile signs for Ravello that point inexorably upwards on the ridge divider between the Minori valley and the coast. ◄ After an archway and chapel, fork L (WNW) on Via della Capella. At the tiny hamlet/lookout extraordinaire of **Torello** (225m, 30min) is the church of San Michele Arcangelo, which incorporates Roman columns.

Orchards and olive groves cover the hillsides, while pretty blue campanulas brighten crannies in the dry stone walls.

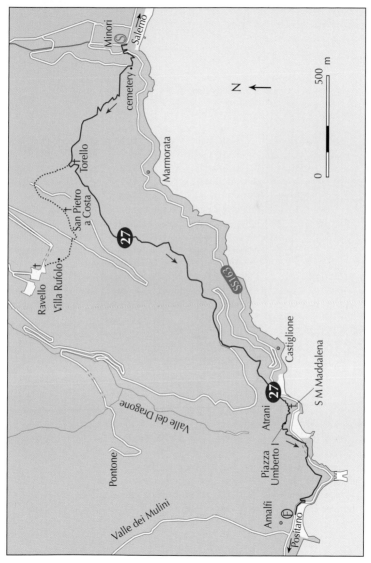

Extension to Ravello (20min)
Continue uphill following clear signs via the church **San Pietro a Costa** and a covered passageway below **Villa Rufolo** to emerge in **Piazza Duomo** at Ravello (359m).

Do take time out to visit the wonderful villas and gardens here before embarking on Walk 25 downhill to Atrani, whence Amalfi.

Brilliant views range to Minori, Maiori, Monte dell'Avvocata and the Gulf of Salerno.

Cultivated and wooded hillsides around Torello

Turn sharp L down Via Torretta Marmorata then R on Via Vallone Casanova, a series of walled staircases between orchards and gardens. Not far on is an unmarked fork (easy to miss) where you need to turn R for a delightful coast through olive groves. ◀ Further along at a white house on a prominent corner go R for what quickly becomes a knee-destroying flight of steps. At last a minor road is reached. Ignoring a descent to Marmorata, turn R for a nearby stepped ramp (signed for Amalfi) which leads around to cross the Ravello road. Only metres uphill is the continuation. With bird's-eye views of **Castiglione** this becomes a wonderful old stone staircase flanking limestone overhangs thick with caper

plants, all the way down to the landmark church Santa Maria Maddalena and its superb terrace immortalised by Escher in a famous lithograph. Backtrack slightly to the flights of stairs and descend to the charming car-free **Piazza Umberto I** in Atrani (1m, 50min), with outdoor cafés. This maze of a village is crammed into the mouth of Valle del Dragone, all but overwhelmed by soaring cliffs. Only metres away is a small beach, on the other side of the raised roadway.

Piazza Umberto I at Atrani

On the opposite side of the square, alongside Osteria Luisella you enter a dark narrow tunnel that emerges between whitewashed houses. Up and up, keep your eyes peeled for rare 'Amalfi' arrows, bearing L (SW) parallel to the main road. As you leave the village the path is edged by a concrete wall and rounds a corner high over a Saracen watchtower. It descends through an atmospheric string of tunnel alleys and steps, finally reaching the road at the E end of the beach not far from the Tourist Office at **Amalfi** (4m, 30min).

WALK 28
Minori and San Nicola

Walking time	3hr
Difficulty	Grade 2
Ascent/Descent	500m/500m
Distance	9.5km/6 miles
Start/Finish	Isabella Hotel, Minori
Access	Minori is a 3km SITA bus trip east of Amalfi on the SS163.

Starting out at the laid-back seaside resort of Minori, this quiet walk climbs fairly steeply through terraced lemon groves and woodland to a scenic ridge and the ruined convent of San Nicola.

Well away from the crowds and glamour of the coast, this route offers a behind-the-scenes glimpse into the rural reality of the area's inhabitants, hard working farming folk who toil on the steep mountainsides with their trusty mules. Lemons are the flavour of the day on the lower slopes, and the path has been dubbed 'Sentiero dei Limoni'. In fact Minori once boasted the largest orchard on the whole of the coast, with an annual production of 250 tonnes. In the Sambuco valley on the return leg are the crumbling ruins of long-abandoned mills, evocative examples of industrial archaeology. Then, at walk's end – before surrendering to the lure of the sea – visit (free of charge) the fascinating remains of the 1st-century Roman villa that has miraculously survived beneath and between modern-day apartment blocks. With mosaic flooring and surprisingly coloured stucco walls, it was one of the so-called maritime villas for Roman nobles the likes of Tiberius.

WALK

On the main road at **Minori** (5m) halfway along the seafront, turn inland at the Isabella Hotel. Facing you is the elaborate cream and yellow facade of **Basilica Santa Trofimena** (an early Christian martyr from Sicily whose ashes washed up ashore here). Walk around the L side of the cathedral, through an archway and up the street

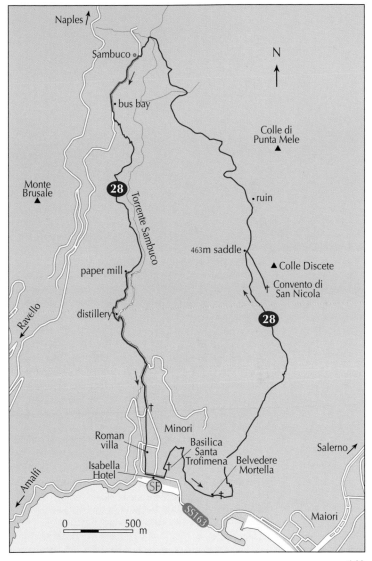

Naples

Sambuco

bus bay

N

Monte
Brusale ▲

Colle di
Punta Mele ▲

28

Torrente Sambuco

• ruin

paper mill

463m saddle •

▲ Colle Discete

† Convento di
San Nicola

distillery

28

Ravello

Roman
villa

Minori

Basilica
Santa
Trofimena

Salerno

Isabella
Hotel

† Belvedere
Mortella

SF

†

Amalfi

SS163

Maiori

0   500 m

Minori's seafront from the path to San Nicola

past a school. A sign for 'Chiesa e convento di S Nicola' points you R up steps. Heading SE between terraced lemon orchards it's a problem-free climb to **Belvedere Mortella** (120m) looking to the beach, as well as Ravello on its lofty platform. Nearby is the church of San Michele Arcangelo (115m) then a level stretch passes the last houses. Ignore the fork for Maiori and veer sharp L uphill between tall stone walls, myrtle, olive and carob trees. In the company of cats and lizards, the stepped path leads N towards the ridge that separates the Minori and Maiori valleys. After a while spreads of chestnut give way to pine woods before you emerge to strawberry trees and rock roses – and views once again. ◄ At a **saddle** (463m, 1hr 15min) in shady wood turn R (SSE) along to the 15th-century **Convento di San Nicola** (484m, 5min), a superbly scenic spot.

San Nicola is visible tantalisingly still far above on its perch.

Return to the **saddle** and continue NNW on the clear path; ahead is **Colle di Punta Mele** high over thickly wooded valleys. At a **ruin** and sign for 'Sentiero Giustino Fortunato', take the L branch though wood. About 20min on, just after a side stream, make sure you keep L at a fork. (Note: should you miss this turn-off, fear not as with a little attention you'll end up in the upper part of the village of Sambuco and can pick up the main route on the road). Grape vines line the stepped way down across a stream, then it's up to the road in quiet rural **Sambuco** (450m, 45min).

Turn L for about 5min to a SITA stop (runs to Ravello are infrequent) then a **bus bay** on the L. Take the concrete ramp in diagonal descent for steep steps zigzagging through well-tended vegetable gardens and past a farm. Ignore turn-offs and keep essentially S through chestnut copses, gradually approaching the stream and the valley floor. ▶ At a large **paper mill** (*cartiera*), long derelict, the road is joined, past a busy limoncello **distillery**. A little further on, after an intersection with a shrine to Santa Trofimena, take Via S Lucia. This pedestrian-only alley will bring you out at a road – on the other side is the **Roman villa**. Only metres away is the seafront of **Minori** (5m, 50min), where cafés galore cater to the thirsty, and that agonising decision awaits walkers: indulge first or slip into the sea for a reinvigorating swim!

Old channelling and abandoned mills line the way, evocative places.

The path through old industrial mills above Minori

WALK 29

Santuario dell'Avvocata

Walking time	4hr 30min
Difficulty	Grade 2+
Ascent/Descent	860m/860m
Distance	9km/5.6 miles
Start/Finish	Reginna Palace Hotel, Maiori
Access	Maiori stands at the intersection of the coast road SS163 with the SS373 that crosses the mountains to Pagani. SITA bus services serve both.

A strenuous and lengthy climb sets out through terraced orchards that soon give way to mountainsides cloaked with aromatic maquis shrubs and shady wood.

All in all this is a beautiful walk worlds away from the crowded coast. The destination is visible from the bustling seaside town of Maiori, where the walk begins. The Santuario dell'Avvocata is an old church and convent complex high on the eponymous mountain. Way back in 1489 a mystical dove appeared to a shepherd and led him to a cave where none other than the Holy Mother awaited. She ordered him to erect a sanctuary in her honour, and in exchange vowed to be his mediator. The place became a full-blown monastery in the 1600s; nowadays though uninhabited it is under the care of the Benedictine friars from Cava de' Tirreni. The buildings are a bit shabby but occupy a stunning spot with a great outlook. Each year on the Monday following Pentecost, festive processions make the big trek bearing statues and picnics (the remnants of which unfortunately litter the slopes). Helicopters ferry up authorities and elderly.

A number of springs with deliciously cool water are found along the trail, but don't forget picnic supplies as the climb is a great hunger stimulant. Maiori has plenty of shops and bakeries. Two diversions from the outward loop add variety to the return.

Santuario dell'Avvocata

WALK

Midway along the seafront of **Maiori** (5m) turn inland at the **Reginna Palace Hotel** onto shop-lined **Corso Reginna**. ▶ Not far along turn R on Via Casa Mannini. Where it ends cross over and continue diagonally L past a school on traffic-free Via De Iusola. This quickly becomes a stepped way passing under an atmospheric covered archway-cum-shrine. Fork R up Via Grade dei Pezzi past a plaque in memory of Maiori's long-gone Jewish community. The gradient steepens considerably between tall walls concealing homes and gardens. Keep R on Via San Vito leading out of the residential area and into light wood up a side valley alive with birdsong. A level stretch overlooking the coast is followed by a staircase fitted with a clever goods lift. At a stuccoed **pink house** is a junction (220m, 30min) where the lower return loop slots in (and Walk 30 proceeds E). Fork L past olive groves and vineyards as the path ENE finally levels out a little. However the mountain awaits and the sanctuary has been in view for a while. A black water pipe and stone channelling accompany the clear path slightly to the R of the natural line of the crest. Two derelict houses are left behind amid thick maquis shrubs and a stream is crossed, over halfway now. Cool holm oak cover is a constant to the ruins of the

Ahead is the spread of the castle San Nicola de Thoro with extensive fortifications.

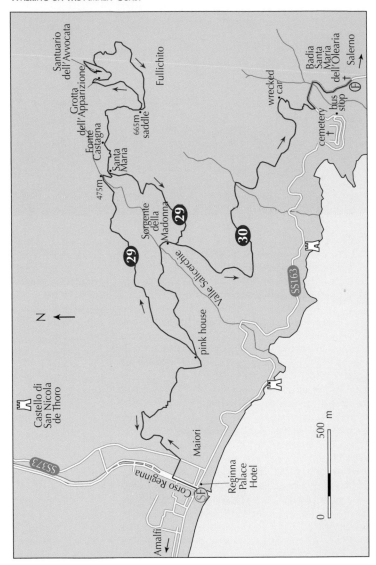

former convent farm **Santa Maria** (500m), with a cross and picnic table.

Keep straight on uphill to an old lime kiln then a stepped way to a spring, Fonte Castagna. The next useful landmark is a **665m saddle** with benches in chestnut wood. Ignore the R fork as it is the return loop, and stick to the main path L. This entails following red waymarks NE up to a limestone overhang as the path curves past the **Grotta dell'Apparizione** (see legend above) and up to the enclosure with the **Santuario dell'Avvocata** (865m, 2hr). ▸

Once you've got your breath back and enjoyed your lunch, from the entrance portal retrace your steps along the wall to a tap, then fork L onto a stony but clear path. At the next junction leave the good path (signed for Maiori) and go L onto a fainter path marked with red spots. Through a ruined gateway this joins a clearer path that descends mostly S and W in curves through vast slopes of ferns over **Fullichito** and past a rock face. After a tree with a madonna image it quickly reaches the **665m saddle** (20min).

Wonderful panoramas space over the gulf busy with motor boats and ferries, and over the Monti Lattari.

The path proceeds through woodland to the sanctuary

Lower down at the **Santa Maria** junction (500m) go diagonally L (SW) on a well-maintained stepped path through shady oak and the occasional garden. About 15min downhill keep R at a fork to snake down a cool gully to the dirt road, only metres from **Sorgente della Madonna** (270m, 55min).

Turn R (SW) mostly on a level at the foot of craggy limestone cliffs. Ignore a track off R and follow the paved lane and its concrete wall through lemon terraces and huts. It ends at a column decorated with a ceramic tile depicting San Vito. A path takes over through grape vines to reach the **pink house** junction (220m, 15min). From here on you retrace the opening part of the walk back to the seafront at **Maiori** (5m, 30min) for a well-earned rest.

WALK 30
Badia Santa Maria dell'Olearia

Walking time	1hr 30min
Difficulty	Grade 1–2
Ascent/Descent	270m/140m
Distance	5.3km/3.3 miles
Start/Finish	Reginna Palace Hotel, Maiori seafront/S Maria dell'Olearia
Access	See Walk 29

This straightforward peaceful walk out of the seaside town of Maiori climbs past the ingenious terraces that groan under the weight of lemons and grapes to a tiny roadside church, Santa Maria dell'Olearia.

Though it doesn't climb anything as high as the Santuario dell'Avvocata (Walk 29), with which it shares the opening half hour, there's still a guarantee of lovely panoramas along the beautiful coast and the Gulf of Salerno on this walk. The walk destination, Santa Maria dell'Olearia, is named after the olive groves here. Benedictine monks founded an abbey here in 973 on the site of an oil press. Half built into the rock face, it has precious ancient frescoes; however it is only usually open Sun afternoons – info ☎ 339 5803486. Even if the church is unvisitable the walk is still worth doing. At the end, either retrace your

The track high above the sparkling sea

steps, not an unpleasant prospect (a further 1hr 30min), or wait at the cemetery for the SITA bus back to Maiori – armed with a ticket obtained in advance.

WALK

Midway along the seafront of Maiori (5m) turn inland at the **Reginna Palace Hotel** onto **Corso Reginna**, lined with shops. Ahead is the castle San Nicola de Thoro with its extensive fortifications spreading downhill. A short way along turn R onto Via Casa Mannini. At the end cross over and walk diagonally L past a school on traffic-free Via De Iusola, which quickly becomes a stepped way. After an atmospheric covered archway-cum-shrine fork R up Via Grade dei Pezzi past a plaque about the local Jewish community, long gone. The going becomes steeper as you pass between tall walls and gardens. Keep R on Via San Vito, leaving the residential area and entering light wood in a side valley alive with birdsong. After a level stretch overlooking the coast is a staircase with a goods lift. Up at a stuccoed **pink house** is a junction (220m, 30min) where Walk 29 to the Santuario dell'Avvocata forks uphill L.

At the elusive turn-off, with views to Montepertuso

Keep straight ahead (NE) along the terraces, high above the tortuous coast road. After water storage basins and a column shrine commemorating San Vito, the path widens to a motorable lane, providing access for the farmers who tend citrus orchards. Curving across wooded **Valle Salicerchie** S beneath craggy limestone cliffs, an old house with drinking water, **Sorgente della Madonna**, is reached (270m).

Further on a turn-off branches gently uphill L, accompanied by drier maquis vegetation dominated by scented broom and rock roses, not to mention lovely sea views. ◄ An outcrop is rounded directly above the town cemetery and a matter of minutes later, immediately after a curve R, is a **wrecked car** near a hut surrounded by prickly pear plants – here you need to branch R off the lane. Take care as it's easy to miss. With views to the Saracen watchtower Torre di Badia on the coast below, the faint path winds downhill, aided by the odd wooden step. As it bears R and improves, yellow waymarks appear. Past an old lime kiln the busy SS163 road is reached. Taking care not to get run over, turn L and walk the remaining 300m to where **Badia Santa Maria dell'Olearia** (130m, 1hr) shelters under an overhang. Alternately go R towards the **cemetery** for the **bus stop**.

Overhead on the southern side of Monte dell'Avvocata the cross of the famous sanctuary can be spotted, whereas due E are jagged rock points and Montepertuso (not to be confused with the one above Positano) with its trademark hole.

APPENDIX A
Italian–English Glossary

acquedotto	water supply, pipe
agriturismo	rural property offering meals and/or accommodation
albergo	hotel
alimentari	grocery shop
aliscafo	high speed ferry, hydrofoil
autobus	bus
autostazione	bus station
badia	abbey
bagni	baths
baia	bay
belvedere	lookout
biglietto dell'autobus	bus ticket
bivio	junction
bosco	wood
buco	hole
cala	cove
calcara	lime kiln
cappella	chapel
cartiera	paper mill
caserma	military barracks, hut
cava	stream, valley, quarry
centro storico	old town centre
chiesa	church
duomo	cathedral
entrata/uscita	entry/exit
eremo	hermitage
faro	lighthouse
fermata dell'autobus	bus stop
ferrovia	railway
fonte, sorgente	spring (water)
forte, fortino	fort, small fort
frana	landslide
frazione	hamlet or village
funicolare	funicular railway
funivia	cable-car
grotta	cave
marina	marina, beach
mulattiera	mule track
municipio	town hall
museo	museum
nuovo/vecchio	new/old
orario	opening times; timetable
ospedale	hospital
palazzo	palace
parcheggio	car park
pedonale	pedestrian
percorso	route
piazza	village or town square
pineta	pine wood
piscina	pool, swimming pool
pizzo	peak, point
(non) potabile	(not) drinkable
previsioni del tempo	weather forecast
proprietà privata	private property
punta	rocky point
resti, ruderi	ruins
rio	stream
scalinata	staircase
scoglio	rock, usually on seafront
seggiovia	chair lift
sentiero	path
spiaggia, lido	beach
sponda	embankment, river bank
stazione ferroviaria	railway station
terme	spa
torre	tower
traghetto	ferry
trattoria	restaurant
treno	train
via	road, street

APPENDIX B
Walk Summary

Walk	Walk Time	Distance	Ascent/Descent	Grade
1	3hr 15min	9.3km/5.7 miles	327m/770m	2
2	1hr 45min	5.5km/3.4 miles	300m/190m	1–2
3	1hr 45min	6.7km/4.2 miles	150m/165m	1
4	2hr	5.3km/3.3 miles	230m/270m	2
5	2hr 30min	5km/3.1 miles	65m/140m	2
6	3hr 30min	6km/3.7 miles	460m/560m	3
7	2hr	5.5km/3.4 miles	160m/160m	1–2
8	1hr 45min	4km/2.5 miles	120m/120m	1–2
9	3hr 45min	11.3km/7 miles	530m/530m	2–3
10	1hr 10min	3km/1.8 miles	100m/100m	1–2
11	1hr 45min	4.6km/2.8 miles	320m/320m	2
12	3hr	7.5km/4.6 miles	510m/510m	2–3
13	2hr 45min	5.1km/3.2 miles	250m/250m	2
14	2hr 30min	4.5km/2.8 miles	390m/390m	2
15	1hr 40min	4km/2.5 miles	220m/220m	1–2
16	4hr 10min	8.5km/5.3 miles	640m/720m	1–2
17	3hr	7km/4.3 miles	550m/550m	2
18	3hr 10min	9km/5.6 miles	310m/795m	2
19	3hr 20min	6.7km/4.2 miles	500m/500m	2
20	2hr 45min	6.5km/4 miles	320m/320m	2
21	2hr 40min	6.5km/4 miles	450m/450m	2
22	4hr 15min	10.5km/6.5 miles	620m/620m	2
23	2hr 10min	6km/3.7 miles	260m/260m	1–2
24	1hr 30min	3km/1.8 miles	150m/150m	1–2
25	1hr 15min	3.5km/2.2 miles	350m (descent only)	1–2
26	2hr 30min	7km/4.3 miles	350m/350m	1–2
27	1hr 50min	4.2km/2.6 miles	250m/250m	1–2
28	3hr	9.5km/6 miles	500m/500m	2
29	4hr 30min	9km/5.6 miles	860m/860m	2+
30	1hr 30min	5.3km/3.3 miles	270m/140m	1–2

APPENDIX C

Further inspiration

So many creative spirits found inspiration here that preparation – or follow-up – for a trip to this area ranges over books, films, painting and music. Dutch engraver MC Escher spent prolonged periods in southern Italy working on his stunningly original lithographs. Richard Wagner found inspiration at Ravello for Parsifal, as did Edvard Grieg for Peer Gynt, while DH Lawrence wrote much of Lady Chatterley's Lover there. The recent French film *Villa Amalia* starring Isabelle Huppert was filmed on Ischia.

Suggestions for inspirational reading include:

* *Siren Land* by Norman Douglas (1911)
  An enchanting if 'purple prose' account of the region at the turn of the 19th century.
* *The Story of San Michele* (1929) by Axel Munthe
  Although largely autobiographical, this also gives an idea of life on Capri during the restoration of his famous villa at Anacapri.
  Helpful flower identification guides are:
* *Flowers of the Mediterranean* by Oleg Polunin and Anthony Huxley (Chatto & Windus)
* *Wild Flowers of the Mediterranean* by Marjorie Blamey and Christopher Grey-Wilson (A&C Black).

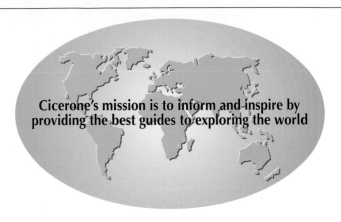

Cicerone's mission is to inform and inspire by providing the best guides to exploring the world

Since its foundation 40 years ago, Cicerone has specialised in publishing guidebooks and has built a reputation for quality and reliability. It now publishes nearly 300 guides to the major destinations for outdoor enthusiasts, including Europe, UK and the rest of the world.

Written by leading and committed specialists, Cicerone guides are recognised as the most authoritative. They are full of information, maps and illustrations so that the user can plan and complete a successful and safe trip or expedition – be it a long face climb, a walk over Lakeland fells, an alpine cycling tour, a Himalayan trek or a ramble in the countryside.

With a thorough introduction to assist planning, clear diagrams, maps and colour photographs to illustrate the terrain and route, and accurate and detailed text, Cicerone guides are designed for ease of use and access to the information.

If the facts on the ground change, or there is any aspect of a guide that you think we can improve, we are always delighted to hear from you.

Cicerone Press
2 Police Square Milnthorpe Cumbria LA7 7PY
Tel: 015395 62069 Fax: 015395 63417
info@cicerone.co.uk www.cicerone.co.uk

CICERONE